Create an effective LinkedIn profile to achieve your goals

The keys to stand out and being visible.

First Edition 2017

Published by David Martínez Calduch

All rights reserved: David Martinez Calduch

ISBN-13: 978-1977559999

ISBN-10: 1977559999

Layout and management for commercialization on Amazon:

The total or partial reproduction of this work by any means or procedure, whether already existing or developed in the future, including reprography and IT processing, and the distribution of copies of this edition through rent or public loans, is strictly forbidden, without prior written permission from the Copyright holders.

Infringement of the aforementioned rights may constitute crime against intellectual property (Art. 270 and successive of the Criminal Code).

SUCCESS IS NOT AN ACCIDENT.

It is hard work, perseverance, learning, study, sacrifice and, above everything else, love for what you do.

- Pele

Acknowledgements

This book is the accumulation of knowledge gathered through study and practice in countless hours, to get go find out what are the right and most effective actions, in every work and project conducted for my company and for the clients, to whom I'm grateful for their confidence in me, and all the knowledge they have provided to me.

David Martínez Calduch

About the author

David Martínez Calduch

Social Selling and Digital Strategy Consultant.

Founder of 3 companies, trainer and international lecturer.

More than 25 years' experience in Information and Communication Technologies.

Executive MBA ESIC Business and Marketing School

Digital Transformation of the organizations.

Writer of several books:

http://amazon.com/author/davidmcalduch

28 years as in company trainer, Business Schools and Universities, in Spain and LATAM. Hootsuite Solution Partner, Hootsuite Ambassador, ECC Evernote Certified Consultant.

Press appearances www.davidmcalduch.com/prensa

More information on:

- **email**: dmartinez@solucionafacil.es
- **LinkedIn**: https://es.linkedin.com/in/davidmcalduch
- **Twitter**: https://twitter.com/davidmcalduch
- **Websites**: https://www.solucionafacil.es
  https://www.davidmcalduch.com
- **Podcast**: https://davidmcalduch.com/podcast

Introduction

After signing up in LinkedIn on 2007, and using it intensively for business since 2009, I've been able to verify firsthand the huge potential that hides within LinkedIn.

During all these years, I've given lectures, seminars, and workshops where I've shown how to get the maximum out of LinkedIn, to achieve the objectives that each of us set for ourselves.

These objectives can be getting clients, distributors, partners, investors, improving our personal brand, looking for a job, etc.

2011 LinkedIn conference in Castellón Commerce Chamber to more than 300 businessmen.

After these years imparting training, conducting LinkedIn consultancy to companies and directors, and carrying out content and advertising campaigns on LinkedIn, I've taking the step to condense mi acquired knowledge, through a series of books that cover the different work areas of LinkedIn, and I've named that series "The Keys of LinkedIn".

https://thekeysof.com/linkedin/

The first book of this series is this one, whose objective is to explain to you, in clear and detailed manner, how to create a LinkedIn profile that if focused on the objectives you pursue, and that will help you achieve them.

It's not a theoretical book; quite the opposite, my advice is that you must have the book right next to your computer and work as you read and put it into practice.

The book starts from moment 0, which is when you sign up on LinkedIn, and ends when you have a complete profile created, and we start to generate our own contact list, looking for people and contacting them. I deal with all of this on the next book.

One of the things that surprises students and clients the most when they come to my lectures or when I meet with them, is when they see LinkedIn's real size, that's the reason why you'll see that this book has over 220 pages, and in it I only explain how to make a good LinkedIn profile.

When one dives in LinkedIn is when one sees the real size it has, and that huge amount of information I have to transmit to you is the reason I've decided to divide it in several books, for it to be a lot more manageable for you at the time of implementing it, in a gradual and structured way.

Within this series, I start the journey with the simultaneous publication of the first two books, which cover the following parts:

- **Create an effective LinkedIn profile to achieve your objectives**
    o In this book, you'll see all of the profile planning and creation, which is the corner stone of every work strategy on LinkedIn. We'll also see security topics and common issues, and how to solve them. Everything you do in LinkedIn is based on the good work you have done here.
- **Get to reach the right people with LinkedIn**
    o In this book, I cover the contact network management, as well as the ways to contact, strategies, advanced searches, how to bypass limitations, and Sales Navigator. The effectiveness of that book is mainly rooted on what you've done with this one first.

For you to easily access the web addresses that will appear in the book, and so it's easier for you to type them, I'll include a QR code in each one of them, for you to scan. Next, I put two free apps, one for Android and the other for iOS, for you to scan the QR codes.

Android	iOS
QR Code Reader	Quick Scan - QR Code Reader
http://ow.ly/Yu2f30eyjCQ	http://ow.ly/J1Mb30eyjFx

Index

Chapter 1 19

Why do I need LinkedIn 19
    1.1 What is LinkedIn 20
    1.2 What Can I Achieve with LinkedIn 24
    1.3 My opinion after 9 years using LinkedIn 25
    1.4 Where is the limit 27
    1.5 Work areas 28

Chapter 2 31

Your Digital Career and Experience 31
    2.1 Social Selling, the new way of selling 33
    2.2 What is Personal Branding 34

Chapter 3 35

Introduction to LinkedIn 35
    3.1 Previous work, documents to prepare 36
    3.2 Signing up in LinkedIn step by step 39
    3.3 LinkedIn on your Smartphone 43
    3.4 What's a LinkedIn profile 44
    3.5 LinkedIn's General View 45
    3.6 Main Menu 46

Chapter 4 49

Profile – Header Image 49
    4.1 LinkedIn's Profile Structure 49
    4.2 The Header Image 54
    4.3 Creating our Customize Header Image 56
    4.4 Corporate Strategies for a Header Image 58

Chapter 5 59

Profile – Contact Card 59
    5.1 What and which is your Objective 60
    5.2 The Profile Picture, Everything You Have to Keep in Mind 61

  5.2.1 Photo's Characteristics, Mistakes, and Advice 62
  5.2.2 LinkedIn's Photo Advice 66
  5.2.3 The New Photo Editor 67
  5.2.4 The New Photo Editor for Smartphones 69
 5.3 The Professional Title with SEO **71**
 5.4 Current Position and Studies **75**
 5.5 The Benefit of the Location and Sector **75**
 5.6 The Summary **76**
  5.6.1 What an Summary is NOT 78
  5.6.2 What is a Summary? 78
  5.6.3 How to Plan and Manage our Summary 79
  5.6.4 Designing our Summary 81
  5.6.6 Creation of Contents 91

Chapter 6 95

Profile – Activity and Results 95
 6.1 Statistics of our Actions **96**
 6.2 Visits to your Profile **96**
 6.3 Posts Visualizations **98**
 6.4 Search Appearances **102**
 6.5 Articles and Activity Box **103**

Chapter 7 105

Slideshare 105
 7.1 Signing up on Slideshare **105**
 7.2 Account Configuration **107**
 7.3 Creating our Content **110**
 7.4 Uploading Content **119**
 7.5 Publishing Content **120**

Chapter 8 123

Profile – Contact Information 123
 8.1 Structure and Functioning **123**
 8.2 Public Profile Address **126**
 8.3 Analyzing Search Engines' Results **129**
 8.4 Websites **131**
 8.5 Telephone and Address **132**
 8.6 Email/s **133**
 8.7 Twitter Accounts **135**

Chapter 9 139

Profile – Job Positions 139
   9.1 Junior Profile 140
   9.2 Senior Profile 141
   9.3 Structure and Functioning 142
   9.4 Adding Job Positions 143
      9.4.1 Position 145
      9.4.2 Company 145
      9.4.3 Location 147
      9.4.4 Time Period 148
      9.4.5 Description 149
      9.4.6 Media 150
      9.4.7 Diffusion and Saving 151
   9.5 Rearranging Job Positions 151
   9.6 Deleting Job Positions 152

Chapter 10 153

Profile – Education 153
   10.1 Registering Studies 153
      10.1.1 University 155
      10.1.2 Degree 155
      10.1.3 Study Field 155
      10.1.4 Grade 156
      10.1.5 Activities and Societies 156
      10.1.6 Time Period 156
      10.1.7 Description 156
      10.1.8 Media 157
      10.1.9 Sharing and Saving 157
   10.2 I Can't Find my University 157

Chapter 11 159

Profile – Skills and Validations 159
   11.1 Previous Work 162
   11.2 Adding the Section 163
   11.3 Adding Skills, deleting them and Arranging them 164
      11.3.1 Adding Skills 165
      11.3.2 Rearranging 165
      11.3.3 Eliminating Skills 165
      11.3.4 Configuring Validations 166
      11.3.5 Who has Validated me, and Hiding it 167
   11.4 Statistics 168

- 11.5 Managing from a Smartphone 170
  - 11.5.1 Validating Skills 170
  - 11.5.2 Managing our Skills 171
- 11.6 Job Search 173
- 11.7 Preventing Someone from Validating us 174
- 11.8 Doubled Validations 175
- 11.9 Validating and de-validating 175

Chapter 12 177

Profile – Recommendations 177

- 12.1 You Lie more than a LinkedIn Recommendation 178
  - 12.1.1 The Bad Use of Recommendations 178
  - 12.1.2 The Good Use of Recommendations 179
- 12.2 How to Request One Step by Step 179
- 12.3 How to do a Recommendation 181
- 12.4 Managing Recommendations 182
  - 12.4.1 Received 182
  - 12.4.2 Given 183
- 12.7 Moving Recommendations 184
- 12.6 Difference between Validations and Recommendations 184

Chapter 13 185

Profile – Accomplishments 185

- 13.1 How to Add Accomplishments Sections 186
- 13.2 Courses 187
  - 13.2.1 Adding Courses 188
  - 13.2.2 Modifying Courses 189
  - 13.2.3 Eliminating Courses 189
  - 13.2.4 Arranging Courses 189
- 13.3 Publications 190
  - 13.3.1 Adding Publications 190
  - 13.3.2 Modifying and Eliminating Publications 191
  - 13.3.3 Changing the Order of the Authors 191
- 13.4 Certifications 192
- 13.5 Honors and Awards 193
- 13.6 Organizations 193
- 13.7 Languages 194
- 13.8 Projects 194
- 13.9 Patents 194
- 13.10 Test Scores 195

13.11 Volunteering 195
13.12 Interests 196

Chapter 14 197

Profile in Several Languages 197
14.1 Available Languages 197
14.2 Creating your Profile in another Language 199
14.2 Eliminating Languages 200

Chapter 15 201

Types of Premium LinkedIn Accounts 201
15.1 Job Search 203
15.2 Companies 203
15.3 Sales 204
15.4 Hiring 205

Chapter 16 207

Job Search 207
16.1 Being on the Search without my Boss Knowing 207
16.2 How Many Job Offers Are There 209
16.3 Analyzing Salaries 210

Chapter 17 211

Safety and Privacy 211
17.1 How Other People See Me when I Visit Them 211
17.2 Access to your Contact List 215
17.3 Other Profiles like Yours 217
17.4 In which Devices do you have LinkedIn Connected 219
17.5 Where is my LinkedIn Account Connected 221

Chapter 18 223

Frequent Problems and their Solutions 223
18.1 I Want to Close a LinkedIn Account 223
18.2 My Company Profile is a Professional Profile 224
18.3 I Have Two Accounts and I Want to Merge Them 224
18.4 I Forgot my Password 226
18.5 I don't remember the Password and can't Access my Email 226
    18.5.1 Using another Email 226

18.5.2 Verifying your Identity 227
18.5.3 Renewing the Password via Mobile 228
18.5.4 Configuring a Mobile 228
18.6 I don't want my Profile to be Public 229

Chapter 19 231

Last Tips 231

Chapter 1

Why do I need LinkedIn

"I hear and I forget. I see and I remember. I do and I understand"

- Confucius

LinkedIn has redefined the way to do business, of interacting between people and of generating synergies. As LinkedIn's merit, I'd highlight that they've been real visionaries in the way how professionals must function and have thus created the perfect tool for such purpose.

In this book you will understand LinkedIn's true potential, and how it can help you achieve your objectives. It's a work on which I have poured the knowledge I have gradually acquired. For the type of book, I've written, you must gradually apply what you learn, so you can get the most out of it.

1.1 What is LinkedIn

LinkedIn is a professional network, unlike other more recreational like Facebook where the goal is to be in touch with friends and acquaintances and sharing cat videos. LinkedIn is focused on professional relationships.

LinkedIn's objective is to create a community for business and job search. Professionals sign up to create their digital presence, to create a reputation and to establish relationships and synergies.

LinkedIn was founded on December 2002 by Reid Hoffman, Allen Blue, Konstantin Guericke, Eric Ly and Jean-Luc Vaillant, and launched on May 2003.

In the Professional Networks market also exist Xing, from Germany, and Viadeo, from France. LinkedIn's strong growth has made it gradually more prominent on the worldwide market.

Since LinkedIn's appearance, it has had very high growth rates.

- 2003 May - LinkedIn is founded
- 2007 Sept - 14,000,000 members
- 2009 Oct - 50,000,000 members
- 2010 Feb - 60,000,000 members
- 2010 Jun - 70,000,000 members
    - and 1,000,000 company profiles
- 2010 Nov - 85,000,000 members
- 2011 Feb - 100,000,000 members
- 2013   > 300,000,000 members
- 2017   500,000,000 members

The breaking point was produced from 2009, where LinkedIn's growth became meteoric, going from 14 million professionals to 85 million in only 3 years and, from there, more than 300 million on 2013, and 500 million on 2017.

Chapter 1: LinkedIn Profile 21

https://blog.linkedin.com/2017/april/24/the-power-of-linkedins-500-million-community

In 2010, when company's profiles were launched, we could see how companies turned to sign up and creating company's profiles.

LinkedIn's growth has been very fast due to the international crisis situation, and the professionals' need to find a job and getting clients.

But this growth will continue to be unstoppable for this reason, university graduates sign in on their last year of school to find a job. Thus, sign in rates are going to be constant, and the introduction rates in society are still very low, many people still don't know LinkedIn, or have heard of it but don't know the potential it has to help them in their objectives.

For example, we have Facebook with 1.94 billion active users a month[1], so, as people say, there's still a long way to go.

June 13, 2016, Microsoft conducted the purchase of LinkedIn for 26.2 billion dollars, now the integration with Office 365 and Microsoft Dynamics CRM is being produced.

A common mission centered on empowering people and organizations

Empower every person and every organization on the planet to achieve more.

Connect the world's professionals to make them more productive and successful.

Connecting the professional world

1+ Billion
Microsoft Users

467+ Million
Members

Creating more connected, intelligent and productive experiences

https://blog.linkedin.com/2016/06/13/microsoft-and-linkedin

---

1 https://en.wikipedia.org/wiki/Facebook

Chapter 1: LinkedIn Profile

LinkedIn has been defined by being always renovating and improving the platform. Since being acquired by Microsoft, a substantial switch has been performed LinkedIn's every function and mode of operation.

Apparently, in a first glance it can seem like it has been visual, but the great switch has been in LinkedIn's working methodology and way of usage.

It's about a LinkedIn where the way of taking full advantage of it is now different from the version before 2017.

LinkedIn's slogan is "Relationships Matter", and here we have one of LinkedIn's keys already.

I work with many Executives that are interested in improving their personal brand, looking for a new job, and see LinkedIn as a handicap. And I'm going to tell you the same thing I tell them, you know the most important things: your professional career, your experiences, your knowledge, your abilities, and we can transfer all of that and use LinkedIn for your benefit. You have the hard part covered, which takes years of work to achieve, and now we only have to transfer it to a new environment; a digital environment in this case.

For course you need to learn to use it, but I repeat, you'll see it's very easy, that's what this book and series are for. If you put what I'm going to teach you in practice, you'll see that once you learn, everything is easier in this life.

The great advantage you'll find with this book series is that the vast majority of people on LinkedIn do what they do because they have learned it by trial and error, they haven't been professionalized, they haven't been trained in its usage, and that's a great advantage. As I usually say in this case, the whole field is green.

1.2 What Can I Achieve with LinkedIn

Here's the key of LinkedIn, what can it help you with, what is it for, but in your concrete case. This aspect is one of the great "mysteries" with people, what makes people in LinkedIn not use it anymore, or people to not sign up, thinking that LinkedIn is only a platform to find a job when they need it, which it actually is, but it's only one of its possibilities:

- Professional career
    - Being in contact with workmates and study partners.
    - Getting a job.
    - Increasing your professional reputation / personal brand, improving your image within the company.
    - Getting clients.
- Company
    - Giving the company visibility.
    - Giving a wider broadcast to its message.
    - Increasing sales.
    - Attracting talent.
    - Exporting / Internationalizing.
    - Locating Distributors / Partners.
- Startup
    - Making your project known.
    - Getting investors.
    - Hiring experts.

These are only a few of the uses you can give LinkedIn, and here's the most important question: what do YOU want to achieve?

1.3 My opinion after 9 years using LinkedIn

Every once in a while, I meet with executives and entrepreneurs who tell me LinkedIn doesn't work for them. That they have been registered for years, that they have many contacts, but in the end, they don't get to generate business.

Being registered in a site doesn't automatically mean that results will be achieved, this would be the same as saying that, simply for making business cards we're going to be selling more. A very simplistic vision.

And the same thing occurs on LinkedIn. These very same professionals, when I check their profiles, the actions they perform and the strategies they're carrying out, I can corroborate they're on a very basic level, both on their profiles creation (a critical piece) as in this tool's usage.

So, I've decided to write this book, with the objective of explaining to you how fabulous this look called LinkedIn is, and what results we have achieved in our company. I could also explain several success cases with our clients, to whom we've performed LinkedIn projects, sales generation, candidates engaging, and internationalization projects, among other things.

I've been using LinkedIn since October 2007, and the moment I decided to open my own company on 2009, we stuck with LinkedIn as the key tool to generate business. Since the beginning, we've used LinkedIn in our company as a commercial tool, for generating Leads on a national (Spain) and International level, mainly on C-level.

We've used LinkedIn as a magnet, creating Branding based on our profiles, which helps the company in our sales tunnel, to conduct the generation of Leads and converting them into clients.

We've been able to corroborate how big LinkedIn's potential is by ourselves, which doesn't solely remain within the very social network with its own search engine, but it also helps you establish yourself in the Internet search engines.

This situation has allowed us to get clients, of which, in some cases, it has been them, finding us by making their search, who have called us to hire our services.

For conducting highly technical projects, LinkedIn has allowed us, in a matter of a few hours, to identify, contact, assess and hire the professionals we needed to participate in the project.

We've been using LinkedIn's advertising campaigns platform for a while now, for us and for our clients. It provides such a detailed segmentation level that it has allowed for a Leads generation of a very high value.

In our case, we've been using more advanced Social Selling techniques for a few years, and during this year we've started to incorporate CRM automation processes, and Big Data analysis (Business Intelligence and Data Mining).

In these moments, we're launching an online training platform, since we have clients all over Spain's geography and in different countries, and we want all of them to have access to the training programs we conduct.

https://www.davidmalduch.com

For you to see a bit of the size that LinkedIn has, I'll tell you the course to learn to create a good professional profile is five hours long, which cover LinkedIn's menu where it says profile; the rest of the menus are more hours, like inviting, managing contacts, content publication and curation, groups, etc. All of it, of course, from a business point of view, based on your objectives.

Chapter 1: LinkedIn Profile 27

So, I encourage you to stop your trial and error tests, train yourself, and professionalize LinkedIn's correct usage. Results can be achieved, as you've been able to see. Now it's a matter of taking the decision to start generating them yourself.

By reading this book you have taken the correct decision of forming yourself, but now you have to apply what you see and start noting its effects.

1.4 Where is the limit

Really, the only limit is marked by you. I've been able to prove myself that there's nothing impossible that can be achieved with LinkedIn.

You can literally get to contact and talk with any person, for example I'll name you a few people I have as Level 1 contacts: LinkedIn Spain's President, LinkedIn China's CEO, LinkedIn USA's Vice-president, hundreds of International or Spain's CEOs of great companies and multinationals, thousands of Sales, Managers, Marketing Managers, CIOs, CFOs, etc.

Of course, all of this is done with the work I've been developing, based on the objectives I wished to achieve.

With this explanation I don't want to give you the image that you have to be trigger happy on LinkedIn, far from being the case. You need to plan ahead, mark goals, see your current situation, and see if we're in a situation to enter where you want, or you need to wait. Rushes are bad advisors.

The main column is always your professional profile. With a bad profile, a profile that doesn't generate trust and confidence, all these people would've never accepted me.

That's the reason it's important to make a very good professional profile, which reflects your truth (and nothing but the truth) and your reality, your professional career, and your experience, which is what will make you reach the people that you want to reach.

If your professional career level is not at the necessary level to be able to reach the contacts you want to reach, you only have one option, which is what I did. Work on your professional career until you hit that level. Because when you contact a person, you only have one round, and if you do it wrong, it'll be very hard or nearly impossible to have another chance.

1.5 Work areas

LinkedIn is divided in several areas, in this book we're going to cover the first area, for a logical sense since, for making a simile, it would be the creation of the foundation of the house we wish to build.

In this book, we'll cover the first one, "Professional Profile"

Professional Profile   Company Page

Talent   Mkt & Ads   Sales

Remember that the Professional Profile is the corner stone of everything you're going to see, the uses we can give to our Professional Profile once it's created and well developed are the following:

Chapter 1: LinkedIn Profile

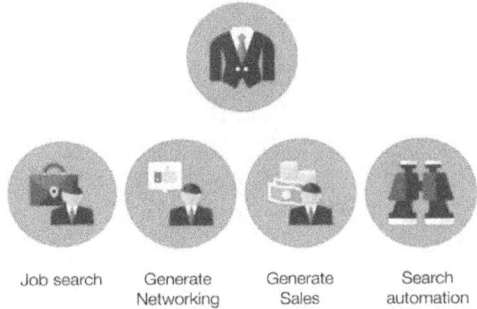

And within the Professional Profile we find the following structure, which is what we'll be working with:

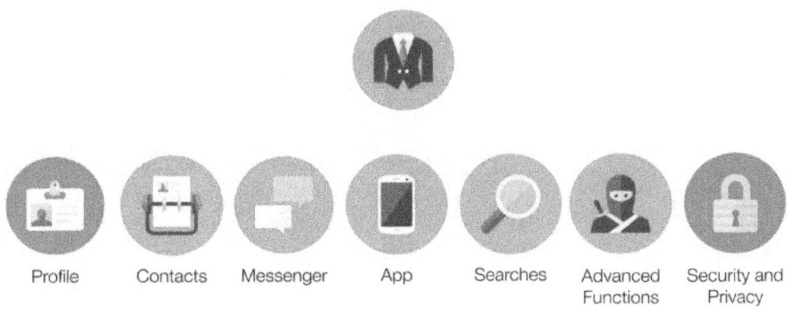

Among these sections, in this book we're going to cover:

- Profile, the complete creation of a LinkedIn Profile.
- App, how to use the Smartphone app.
- Advances features.

In the second book "Get to Reach the Right People with LinkedIn" we'll see:

- Contacts.
- Security and Privacy.
- Messaging.
- Searches, including advanced and automatic searches.

With which, with the two book, we'll have the profile area complete.

Chapter 2

Your Digital Career and Experience

"If you don't have a digital presence in the web, you isolate yourself and nobody remembers you"

Lars Hinrichs, Xing's Founder

Your professional career and your experience are critical. Well used, they'll help you generate confidence with your interlocutor, but the offline world has a limit, the amount of people you can meet, and the hours in a day we can dispose. And here's where the digital world allows us to break that barrier and helps us increase our reach.

If we still don't have a professional career, we have to work toward creating it. The constant effort and time will make you a great professional, remember the bamboo.

When the bamboo is planted, for the first months nothing happens. This happens only during the first seven years, in this time it has been creating a root system, and when the seventh-year hits, in six weeks the bamboo grows over 30 meters tall.

You must think in your professional career in the medium and long term.

This is how people think a professional career is.

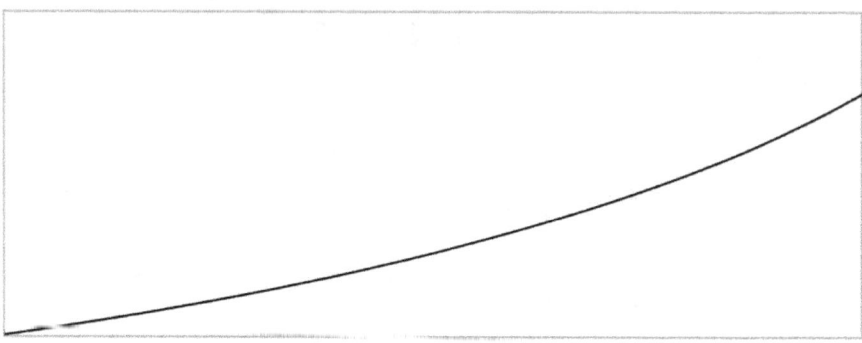

And this is how it really is.

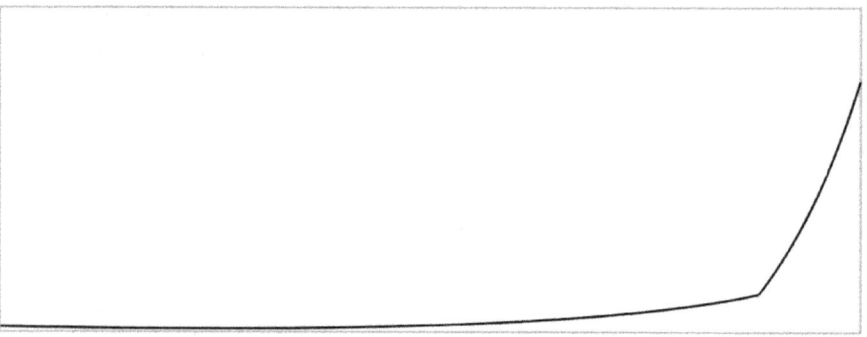

If we want to transmit something that isn't true in the digital world, we'll become the typical deceitful salesman. It's about a personal decision of what we really want to be.

Therefore, we must be very strict and upright, and publish only that which is true. And this doesn't mean we have to publish absolutely everything, we're not on Facebook or any other playful social platform. Here, your professional career is at stakes, as well as your future.

Chapter 2: Your Digital Career and Experience

2.1 Social Selling, the new way of selling

The way of making sales and the very sales funnel has radically changed, LinkedIn is a critical piece in this new sales model. In this section I won't extend myself a lot, since you should only work it when you've finished applying this book and the contacts generation one.

If you want to delve deeper in this section, you can do it in another practical work I've written with Esmeralda Díaz-Aroca that it's available on Amazon.

http://amzn.to/2tg9mLI

2.2 What is Personal Branding

In the new model of making business, we've changed the model, we've been increasingly incorporating technologies and at the same time we've been approaching the human side more.

The old B2C or B2B model has now been simplified to a H2H (human to human) model. If I want to make businesses with a company, I can't speak with a logo, or with a building, we work with a person who represents that company.

If the people I contact or contacts me doesn't transmit confidence, I'll look for another company to give me a solution. And that company, depending on that person, achieves or loses the sale.

So the recognition you have today as a professional in the day-to-day with your peers and clients, we need to transfer it to a digital environment so it helps you on this labor.

This personal digital brand, we're currently working it within company projects in Employer Branding and Employee Advocacy, the companies are noticing the importance of the brands of the professionals that are among their ranks.

So now it's time to start creating your digital presence and brand.

Chapter 3

Introduction to LinkedIn

You need to constantly be reinventing yourself and invest in the future.

- Reid Hoffman, LinkedIn's Cofounder

Now, what we're going to do, is starting to work with LinkedIn. If you've already signed up in LinkedIn, read it anyway to see where you can improve, since I'll show you the methodology I use step by step.

If you still haven't signed up, follow the guide I show you here to do it right from the start.

Now we're going to sign up on LinkedIn and we're going to make a general review of the sections before entering the profile creation.

But before that, you need to do a previous work with which we'll set the foundation of the subsequent work you're going to develop

3.1 Previous work, documents to prepare

Before starting working on your LinkedIn Profile, I always recommend doing a previous work that will help us go faster and more effectively. It's possible you already have done part or all of the work, all the better. But let's go over it to make sure we haven't left anything behind.

✓ Work Life Report

In Spain's case, the Ministry of Social Security (Work) allows you to download an official document where your work life, dates, companies, and job positions you've been in are shown.

http://ow.ly/zJpq30cJtUa

Something similar surely exists in your country.

✓ Curriculum Vitae

One of the things I've always done and recommend is for you to create and update a full CV, which you regularly update with the new tasks you perform, the projects, achievements, etc. This CV is actually for you, to not forget things.

Chapter 4: LinkedIn Profile

If you're starting your professional career, you won't deem that important right now, but I assure you, when you have a few years of experience, sometimes it's hard to remember all of what you've done in each position, as years go by.

I've created a folder in my PC called "CV" where I keep "CV David Martinez Calduch 2017-09", when I modify it in January 2018, I copy the MS Word document (it takes very little space) and rename it to "CV David Martinez Calduch 2018-01". That way, I have a history of changes performed. My advice is for you to make it with MS Word or Evernote, whichever is more practical for you.

✔ Curriculum Vitae for a position

When you have to present yourself for a job position, what you need to do is to create a concrete 1-page long CV for that position, where you highlight your strengths for that position.

You'll do it from your complete CV. To do it you can use Word, or a European CV template you can find in this URL:

https://europass.cedefop.europa.eu/es/documents/curriculum-vitae

Or you can use the free web app www.canva.com. Among their options (desktop version) you have an option to create attractive one-page long CVs. The designs are already created, and you only have to choose which one you want, and fill it with your info.

A simple new way to design

Now, with all of this information gathered, we can start our LinkedIn signup and customization process.

Chapter 4: LinkedIn Profile 39

3.2 Signing up in LinkedIn step by step

To sign up, we're going to follow the process from a PC. If you're going to use a Tablet, I recommend you install the browser Chrome. When you open it in a Tablet and go to www.linkedin.com, in the top right corner you can open a menu and indicate you want to see the website in its Desktop version (PC).

All the work we're going to develop, we're going to do it with our free LinkedIn account. If there's any feature where you need the paid version, I'll let you know, but those will be very isolated issues.

If you had previously signed up to LinkedIn, in the top area you can enter the email and password with which you signed up.

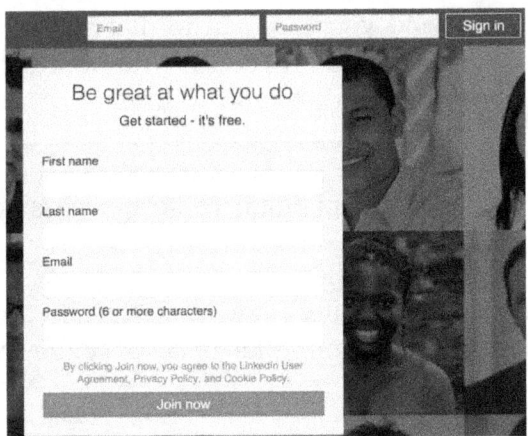

If you can't remember your password, you can request for a new one by entering the email you signed up with. You can do it by following this link: http://ow.ly/BrLs30cJv5I

These are the steps to sign up:

1. We open our browser[2] and we enter
   www.linkedin.com

2. Fill up all the data in a correct manner, don't type it in all caps or all lower case. The email you enter now can be changed later if you wish, don't worry about that. As soon as you sign up, LinkedIn will send you an email to that address for you to verify you're the owner. If you don't, there'll be features you won't be able to use.

So you better use an email you can access now to click on the link.

What LinkedIn will do now is to take us through a tutorial to help us introduce the minimal data to begin creating our digital presence.

---

[2] I recommend Firefox, Opera, Chrome or Safari

Chapter 4: LinkedIn Profile   41

In zip code, use the once corresponding to your job address, not your home, since we're creating a Professional Profile.

Here, it will ask you if you're starting your professional career and have no experience. "Are you a student?" If you have a professional career you must fill in your current position or the latest you've had.

A very important tip is that, if the company's name appears on the list when you type it, as you can see on the example, you must click to select it and link yourself to it. This is a very important point. If it doesn't appear, only the company's legal representative can create the company. In that case, type the name even if it doesn't appear on the list.

Below the company's name, it'll ask you the sector to which you belong.

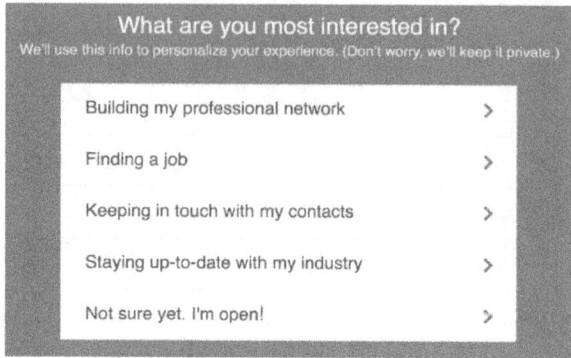

This question is an inner survey they perform to see which usage the people signing up are looking.

This is already the last step, and you have to introduce a numeric code that has been sent to the email you used to sign up.

This is a sample of the email you're going to receive. Once you've entered the code, you'll be registered in LinkedIn.

Chapter 4: LinkedIn Profile

At this point, what LinkedIn will indicate to you is that it's going to help you find the people you already know and have signed up on LinkedIn. It won't invite anyone on its own, that's for you to decide, but it'll help you locate them

By clicking continue, it'll ask for your permission and/or password to browse through your contacts in LinkedIn (it's done through email addresses), in a first screen (Step 1 of 2), it's people you know and are on LinkedIn, my advice is for you to invite whoever you want. And Step 2 of 2, are those people whose emails you have, but aren't on LinkedIn yet, my advice is to not invite anyone and skip this step, or else they'll all contact you to ask you to explain what LinkedIn is to them.

LinkedIn is constantly changing and improving, so it's possible that the assistant has even more questions. Keep responding those you want to respond and skipping those you don't.

3.3 LinkedIn on your Smartphone

Once we've signed up and verified our email, we can install the LinkedIn app in our Smartphone.

Android	iOS
http://ow.ly/jdjZ30eyqbN	http://ow.ly/N7r930eyq6o

When you've installed the App, enter the email you signed up with and the password. During the book we're going to work with the computer and Smartphone, so you know how to use it from both devices.

3.4 What's a LinkedIn profile

Your LinkedIn profile is your presentation, your digital presence, where people can know about you, about your career, your achievements, "what you can do for them."

https://www.linkedin.com/in/davidmcalduch

It's your digital presentation card. When you meet a person or attend an interview, it's very hard, if not impossible, to explain your whole professional career to them. In linked in you can do it and the person visiting your profile can enter in detail if so they wish, and we're also able to include recommendations from our clients and former bosses. All of this, don't you worry, you'll learn how to do it.

Chapter 4: LinkedIn Profile

3.5 LinkedIn's General View

When you enter www.linkedin.com you'll see a screen very similar to this one, which is the new layout that has been remodeled in 2017.

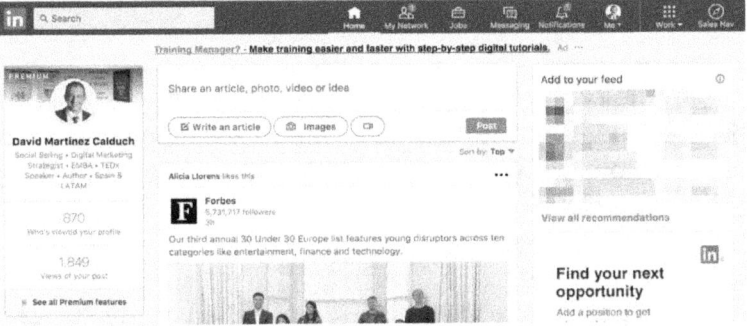

In the top right section, we have the main menu with all the options.

In the left section we can see a box where our picture is shown (once you've set it up) and a series of options.

Now we're going to check each one of these sections, so you have a global vision of the screen.

In the section below your picture, it shows numbers that change, in this case it indicates that 957 people have visited my profile in the last 90 days, and that I have a post that has generated 7,429 views. We can click on any of these two values and we'll go to the corresponding screen to see the data with more detail. If you click on your picture, it'll take you directly to your profile.

![Share an article, photo, or update box with Write an article, Image, and Post buttons]

In the center we have this box where we can post content, for people among our level 1 contacts to see (those who have invited us, or whom we've invited and they've accepted), if they click on Like, comment, or share it, then their level 1 contacts can see it (which are our level 2 contacts).

Under this box, posts being published by our level 1 contacts appear, the people we follow (regardless of their level), and the companies and universities we follow.

In the right section, the information that appears changes: advertisement, contacts that may interest you, etc.

3.6 Main Menu

In the top right section, you have the LinkedIn icon, if you click it you'll go to the home page.

Next to it, we find the people, companies, job positions, groups, and universities search bar.

In the old version, the word "Advanced" appeared next to the search bar so you could go to advanced searches, now this option

Chapter 4: LinkedIn Profile   47

is the magnifying glass you can see next to the word "Search" and by clicking it you enter in advanced options.

In the right section we have the new menu with all the options.

You may have observed that the menus on my LinkedIn are in English, mi advice is for you to work (in the computer) with the English version, since when new options are launched they're immediately available in the English version, and they are gradually introduced for the rest of the languages.

If you want to set it to English, you have to go to this address (you can only do it in a computer).

https://www.linkedin.com/psettings/select-language

Having the menus in English doesn't imply you have to do the profile in English, you can do the profile in the language of your preference.

In the menu bar (from left to right) we have:

1. Home, it's the same as pressing the LinkedIn icon, it'll take us to the home page (the wall).
2. My Network, it's your list of contacts, the people who have invited you and whom you've accepted. The people who are now your level 1, and you're directly connected.
3. Jobs, it's the same as doing an advanced search and selecting Jobs.
4. Messaging, it's a very powerful tool to manage communications like WhatsApp on a business level, without needing to know the other person's phone number or email.

5. Notifications, where it alerts us about new messages, when someone mentions you, etc.
6. Me, it's to access your profile, the configuration options and, under everything, the company pages you manage.

7. And the last one is Work, where we have access to more functions, and the last option is for creating a company page (use it only if you're the company's legal representative).

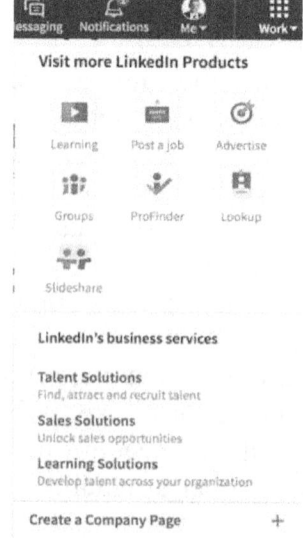

Chapter 4

Profile – Header Image

LinkedIn's visual aspect is very important, as the saying goes, an image is worth a thousand words.

You'll see that the Header Image, when used well, can help you create a more professional image, which can help you deliver the message you want to deliver.

4.1 LinkedIn's Profile Structure

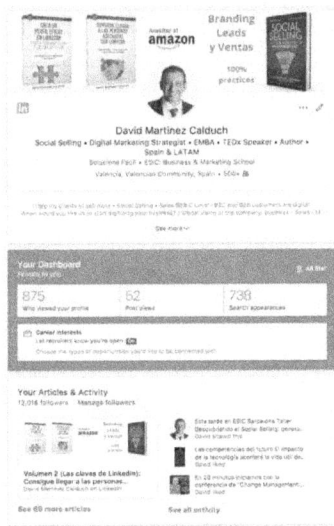

Now let's see LinkedIn's new Profile Structure. It starts with a contact information sheet (this sheet already existed in LinkedIn's previous version), and then there's a notifications zone. Under it, we can see this person's posts.

Next, we have the Experience, where the Job Positions appear (in the new version, only the last 5 positions are visible).

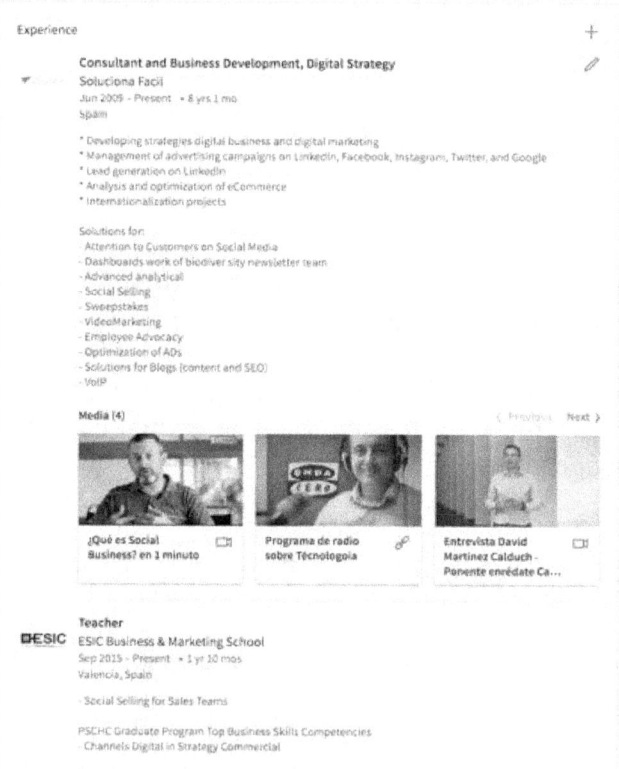

The next section is Education.

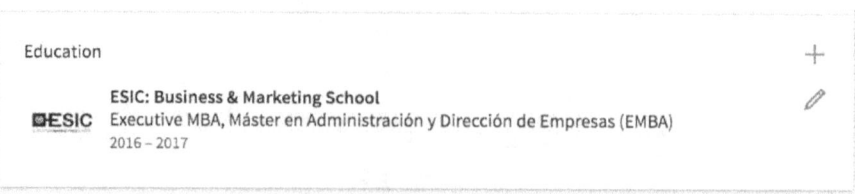

Then there's Skills and Validations, in a compressed version.

Chapter 4: LinkedIn Profile

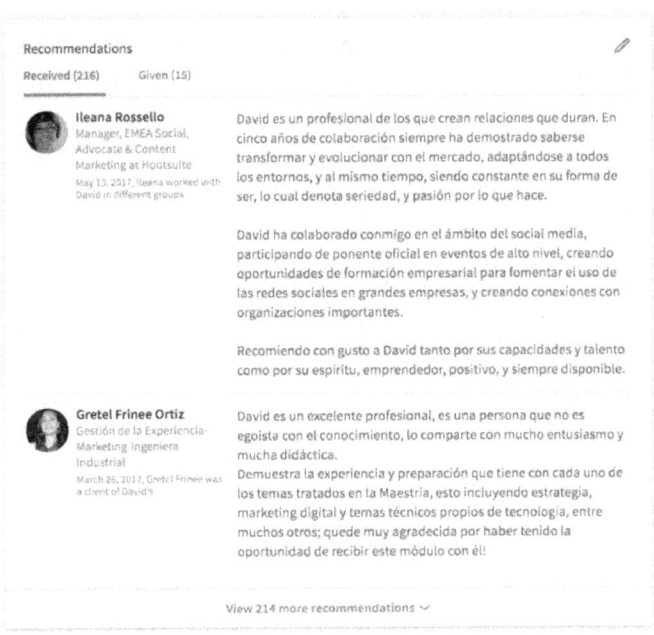

And Recommendations, which is a very important section.

And all the rest of the sections are together in a sole block, where all of them are compressed.

Before, these sections were separated, and it was also allowed to switch them in order and customize the profile's structure much more.

And on the top right section, if we click on "Contact and Personal Info", this screen pops out.

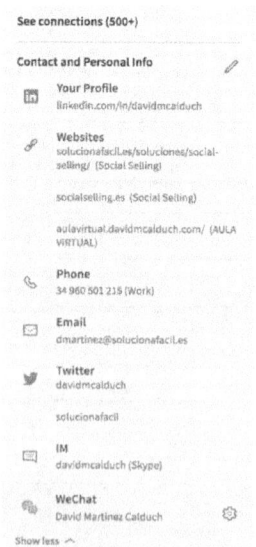

As you'll see now, in the Smartphone, LinkedIn has made it look the same, following the same structure.

Chapter 4: LinkedIn Profile

Points to highlight:

- The structure of every profile is unified for an easier reading.
- Contents are simplified (reduced summary, older posts hidden, etc.) so we can focus on the most recent posts when visiting a profile.
- Upper section with posts and indicators, so we can quickly see which type of content this person posts.

Ultimately, they've aimed for profiles to be easier to read and check at first glance and, if I we're interested, for us to open the sections to enter in more detail.

Now we're going to start working on each one of the parts of a LinkedIn Profile, seeing what we need to do, the possibilities it offers, and which approach we can give to it, depending on what you want to achieve.

4.2 The Header Image

The first section of our profile is a header image we can include. This image will be seen in a computer, as seen in the image above, and also in Smartphones, as seen in the image below.

I'll show you another header image I've used before.

Chapter 4: LinkedIn Profile

    The image's size must be 1584x396px, it can be a JPG or PNG file.

    The objective is giving our profile a more attractive aspect, including a message we're interested in delivering, showing a brand image, etc.

    You can put up a landscape view, an aerial view of your city, the views from your offices, a panoramic view of your facilities, your company's slogan with a one color background, a picture with your team, etc. Mainly, you have to feel comfortable with the image and it mustn't harm you professionally.

    One of the options is searching for an image you like and setting it up. Here's a few websites where you can find one.

https://linkedinbackground.com

In the website's top menu you can select the picture category you want to see.

Here's another website that is also organized by categories.

http://freelinkedinbackgrounds.com

And the last one with the most images.

http://ow.ly/TORw30cKh98

4.3 Creating our Customize Header Image

To create our customized header image we can use www.canva.com (from a computer), which has creativity prepared specially for LinkedIn.

Chapter 4: LinkedIn Profile

Clicking it will open a new window, and on the left section there are many pre-created designs where we only need to select the one we like the most, change the picture, put up our text, and it's done.

By having the design created, you only need to see which one adapts to your idea the most, and from there, try to do the least amount of changes possible, unless you are a designer.

Once it's done, click on the blue Download button, and we can select if we want it on JPG or PNG, we download it to our PC, and we can set it up on our LinkedIn Profile.

I don't recommend you leave LinkedIn's default image, it's a good idea to customize it

4.4 Corporate Strategies for a Header Image

This image, if used well, can be part of our corporate strategy.

 If you want to give a more team-like image, and I don't mean football ;-), you can request your Marketing Department and your whole team to use the same one.

Imagine we're a staff selection company, we could make an image in our company's logo's color and put the text "WE'RE HIRING" or the company's slogan on the center.

It's a zone where we can include the message we want to be heard, the products we sell, the solutions we bring, etc.

Chapter 5

Profile – Contact Card

This zone is very important, because when a person comes visit our profile, it's the first thing they'll see, and in a lot of cases, it can be the only thing they check.

On this summarized card appears the info we're about to introduce, and other information that summarizes other sections of the profile, to show a quick glance without having to go through the whole profile.

This card has also gone through great changes in its usage, and its approach. Now you'll see that the old approach doesn't work anymore, due to this renovation.

5.1 What and which is your Objective

Here we can see how our card looks on a Smartphone.

We can see the header image, our profile picture, our full name and our professional title.

On the line below, we see our latest studies, our location, and the amount of contacts we have.

And lastly, two very short lines explaining what we do.

Thanks to this card, we can quickly know a person's situation, what they do for a living, where they work, etc. and we can decide if we go further in the profile to continue investigating.

Therefore, this section is very important, because it's the one that'll allows to interact with the people in which we're interested.

5.2 The Profile Picture, Everything You Have to Keep in Mind

> *The limit of people we can manage in our brain is 150.*
>
> *- As calculated by Robin Dunbar, evolutional anthropology professor in Oxford University.*[3]

When we enter the digital world, the barrier of the amount of people we know disappears, and our contact list multiplies.

In this moment, my level 1 contact list in LinkedIn has 10,000 contacts, the limit is at 30.000.

---

[3] Source: Forbes Jan-30-2016
https://www.forbes.com/sites/amitchowdhry/2016/01/30/most-facebook-friends-are-not-your-real-friends-says-study

As you can imagine, if we're guided by Professor Robin Dunbar's study, it's a quantity that our brain is not able to manage, and I can truly confirm it is true.

Then, how am I able to locate a person among this extensive list? By their photo. Our brain works with images, we're able to remember the face, and from there we can search for that person and locate them, even if we don't remember their name.

> *Posting your photo on your profile increases your profile visits x21.*
> *– LinkedIn*

So, no doubt, posing a good photo is of the utmost importance.

5.2.1 Photo's Characteristics, Mistakes, and Advice

Any action you want to perform, finding a job, getting clients, etc., when you do it, the other person will see a grey little man (if you haven't uploaded a photo), or you in a photo. Which one to you think will give more confidence?

 The image's size must be 400x400px, it can be JPG, PNG and GIF. Max size is 8MB.

 The objective is to be clearly recognized, and if we meet someone, for them to know it's us at first glance.

Chapter 5: Profile – Contact Card 63

You can do the photo with a blurry background, a landscape, in your offices, with your company's logo behind, in your study, etc.

LinkedIn's rules

- According to LinkedIn's rules, the only thing they demand is that you can be recognized in the photo

- This means you can't set up a photo with a company logo where you don't appear

LinkedIn indicates what should not appear in the photo[4]:

- Company logos

- Landscapes

- Animals

- Words or phrases

- A picture that doesn't resemble you

- A picture that isn't a headshot

Usual mistakes

- Using a wedding photo, doesn't matter if you're an attendant, we can tell.
- Using an ID or passport picture, -0 no comments.

---

[4] Rules LinkedIn uses to make the decision of eliminating a profile picture.

- Using an old pictures, 10 years or older, didn't we tell you we want to be recognized by our photo?
- Taking a picture with your Smartphone and directly upload it to LinkedIn. What's your Smartphone's Camera's resolution? The norm is that when people look at your photo, they can zoom in and count your eyelashes.

My advice for the photo:

- Depending on your sector and your job position, there'll be a dressing protocol. Find profiles like yours to see what is worn in your sector.
- Find a good professional photographer and tell them the picture is for your LinkedIn profile, listen to their advice, and have a photo shoot (my last session was nearly 2 hours long), the end of the session is when you loosen up and take the best photos.
- If you're implementing LinkedIn in your team, organize one or more days with the photographer so he can take pictures of everyone.
- Spare no expenses, that's the first barrier between you and reaching your goals.
- Ask the photographer to let you choose several photos and to send them to you in high quality.
- The photo you choose to use for your LinkedIn Profile, copy it and change the resolution to 400x400px.
- Put your full name in the photo file's name.
- Now you can upload the picture to your profile.
- I usually change the photo every year and half or two years, so I can be recognized exactly as I currently am.

I'll show you some pictures from the last shoot so you can see.

Chapter 5: Profile – Contact Card 65

In my case, the left image was cut by the photographer and it was the one she gave me to use on my LinkedIn Profile, the middle picture, I used it as my last header image and my website www.davidmcalduch.com, and the last one still hasn't been used.

Problems and solutions: If you can't upload the photo

- The image's max size is 20.000x20.000px
- Check that the file's name isn't too long and that it doesn't have any special characters (accents, ñ, ç, periods, dashes, etc.)
- If you work with a computer screen with low resolution, there are buttons like "Save" that aren't seen when you upload the photo (change the screen resolution on Windows http://ow.ly/LVbl30cKxrX).

- Try another browser and check if you have the browser's latest version.
- Still having problems? Reset your computer.

5.2.2 LinkedIn's Photo Advice

Let's see what LinkedIn's official advice is when taking your picture[5]:

- Be aware of your surroundings
    - An uniform background behind you can be a good idea, instead of having many objects behind you (paintings, boxes, etc.) that can make the picture miss its main focus, which is you.
- Use natural light
    - If you're not a photography professional and don't have the right material, it's better if you use natural light, instead of using the flash. Natural light will illuminate your face well and won't cast shadows. But avoid the light hitting you directly.
- Use the right camera
    - You can use a DSLR or a Smartphone, if the latter, try to use a recent one. If possible, use a tripod and the Smartphone's main

---

[5] Source: LinkedIn, how to take a professional selfie

camera, since it's more powerful and will give you a better quality.
- Think of the angle
    o Take the camera or Smartphone and put it up. With this angle you'll highlight your eyes, and will make your head and neck look smaller. If you're aiming for the opposite effect, then lower the camera for the picture.
- Think of what to wear
    o The important thing is you, and you don't want the clothes you're wearing to get more attention than you. Dress accordingly and in a professional manner.
- Don't center yourself
    o In the photo, your eyes must be on one third of the way from the bottom to the top and from either side.
- Be yourself, don't be a cliché
    o Don't smirk or imitate gestures or postures you've seen before. It's better to give a sensation of naturalness.

5.2.3 The New Photo Editor

LinkedIn has launched a new and powerful photo editor both for the Smartphone and desktop versions, with which you can crop the image and put effects on it.

When you're in your profile and click the photo, the photo editor will appear.

You can also enter this address to go straight to the photo editor.

https://www.linkedin.com/profile/edit-picture-info

And you'll reach a screen like this one.

We have three options to edit the picture.

1) Crop, it's the option that is now active and allows us to Zoom in or out, and Straighten it turning it around.

2) Filter, shows us these options to apply effects on the image.

3) Adjust, shows us these options.

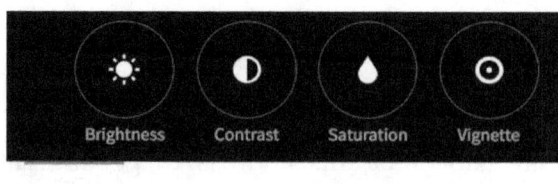

Chapter 5: Profile – Contact Card 69

Below everything, on the right side, we have "Visibility", where we can establish who we want to be able to see our picture.

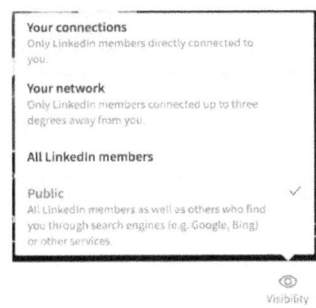

The options are: Only your level 1 contacts; your level 1, 2 and 3 contact networks; every LinkedIn member; and the last one, which is the one I have activated, everyone, including people outside LinkedIn.

Below, you have the button to change the picture, upload it from your computer, and saving all the changes.

5.2.4 The New Photo Editor for Smartphones

This new photo editor has also been incorporated to the Android and iOS Apps. Open the LinkedIn app, touch your photo that appears on the top right section to go see your profile.

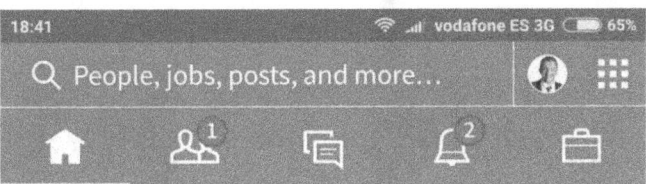

When you enter your profile, you click your photo that appears on the center.

On the top section, you can set the visibility. The buttons to modify it are on the posterior part.

If we click the pencil on the bottom left, we'll enter this screen with the options "Crop", "Filter", and "Adjust".

And if you click the camera icon, you can take a new photo with your Smartphone or upload one from your gallery.

Chapter 5: Profile – Contact Card   71

5.3 The Professional Title with SEO

Now, what we're going to do is click on the blue pencil you can see on the top right part, and the following screen will appear.

Here you can correct the info, if there's any mistake in the names and surname.

The field that goes next is the "Headline" or "Professional Title".

From a simple point of view, whatever goes on your work contract and/or what's on your presentation cards is what you should set as your "Professional Title".

But that's not always the case, and it doesn't need to be, let's see some examples:

- Imagine you're an Economics major, and now you've found a Managerial job. What do we put? What you're doing right now or what you've studied? I'd put up "Economist" since that's your profession, if that's what you want to do for a living.
- Let's think of a person who works in HR, let's suppose they have a "Recruiter" position and deals with ICT profiles, we could put "ICT Profiles Recruiter" "ITC Sector Recruiter" or something along those lines, another option could be, if there is any open position, to add "ICT Sector Recruiter – We're hiring" or "We have open positions. Contact me"

Mistakes to avoid:

- You're a Freelancer an put "VP" or "CEO", it's going to harm you for several reasons; first, because it doesn't adjust to reality, CEO stands for "Chief Executive Officer" and this is what it means https://en.wikipedia.org/wiki/Chief_executive_officer

Chapter 5: Profile – Contact Card

If you put "VP" or "Vice-President" LinkedIn will try to help you know people on your same field and professional level, which would be fake, and therefore you'll lose LinkedIn's potential.

You must keep in mind that when people conduct searches within LinkedIn, is the word they're searching is on your professional title, you have better chances of appearing in the first search results, always keeping in mind the volume of visits you and the other people who appear on the results have, and other SEO factors that LinkedIn analyzes.

Of course, we'll only put that word or words which actually have to do with our professional career and in which we have experience and knowledge.

You must be aware of the great importance the "Professional Title" has, since it's the first thing that people will see, it has to be well designed, clear and direct, it must contain the keyword that you're interested in, and maybe even include a Call To Action (CTA)[6].

When we post content, both in the form of an article or our state, only our photo, full name, and "professional title" are seen.

---

[6] Wikipedia CTA Call to Action – https://en.wikipedia.org/wiki/Call_to_action_(marketing)

Here we can see a post by Tiffani Bova, and we can see her photo, full name (in her case, she has included an icon), and in the bottom line we have her "Professional title".

In this post by Guy Kawasaki, we can see his photo, his full name (the blue icon was put by LinkedIn because he's an influencer), and in the bottom line his "Professional title".

In both cases, if we don't click their photo or name to go check their professional profile, we won't know anything else about them, what they do for a living, etc. That's the importance of a good Title.

5.4 Current Position and Studies

> Current Position
> Consultant and Business Development, Digital Strategy at Soluciona Facil
> Add new position
> Education
> ESIC: Business & Marketing School
> Add new education

Don't touch anything in this section, since this information comes from one of the sections below and we'll see how to put it all up to date. Once we have completed the sections you can come here to select what you want to be shown.

5.5 The Benefit of the Location and Sector

> *Including your locations helps your profile show up 23 times more in searches.*
>
> *- LinkedIn*

The Location and Sector are of vital importance, since this info is used by LinkedIn to introduce us contacts related to our sector and our professional title. The location can be useful when we're looking for a job, since we can indicate how many Km away from us we're interested in finding job offers.

> Country: Spain   ZIP code: 46001
> Locations within this area
> Valencia Area, Spain
> Industry *
> Online Media

5.6 The Summary

> I help my clients to sell more • Global vision of the company: Business - Sales - Marketing - ICT • Social Selling - sales B2B C Level • B2C and B2B customers are digital. When would you like us to start digitizing your business? Org...
>
> See more ⌄

Right at the end of this sheet appears the Summary, one of the most important sections. This section has also had many big changes.

The first thing we can see is that, unlike the previous version of the LinkedIn Profile where the whole summary could be seen, now only the first two lines of the summary are shown.

Here you can see that this also occurs on Smartphones, where it's trimmed even more.

> **David Martinez Calduch**
> Social Selling • Digital Marketing Strategist
> ESIC: Business & Marketing School
> Valencia Area, Spain • 500+ 👥
>
> I help my clients to sell more • Global vision
> of the company: Business - Sales...

If the person visiting us clicks on "See more" on a computer, or on the three small blue dots on a Smartphone (do they even notice that they can click there?), then the whole summary pops out and they can see the rest of the content, as you'll see in the following image.

Chapter 5: Profile – Contact Card

As you can see, you can extend the text a lot more and even include some multimedia content.

Now that you've seen the example of my summary, let's see what a summary isn't, what a summary is, how to approach it, and how to build one based on your objectives.

I have to be honest, this part of the Profile can be the one you'll need to dedicate more time to, because of its importance and the difficulty of being able to summarize the message we want the person visiting us to perceive.

With a summary of at least 40 words it's more likely that you show up on the searches. Make sure you add a bit of your personality, almost 87% of recruiters will look for it.

- LinkedIn

5.6.1 What an Summary is NOT

When setting examples, I always go to the extremes, maybe exaggerating a bit, because it's the best way of quickly noticing the differences and what I want to show you.

What a Summary is NOT:

- It's not about who you are "Hello, I'm Marta, I was born in Barcelona, I'm 37 years old, etc."
- It's not about what you sell "Hello, I sell heavy machinery type xxxx".
- It's not about what you like "I like doing yoga and eating healthy".
- It's not about what you want "I want to reach X volume of business and open Y market".
- It's not about what you're looking for "I'm interested in companies from the XX sector".

We could say that what interests you, as the phrase says, interests you, but this isn't about you ;-) because what we want is to generate interest in the person visiting our profile.

5.6.2 What is a Summary?

Now we need to change the focus, from us to the other person, and that's where the Summary's success lies.

I'm going to say it loud and clear, I personally don't care which products or services you bring, I don't care about what you do. The ONLY thing I care about is:

What can you do for me?

Chapter 5: Profile – Contact Card

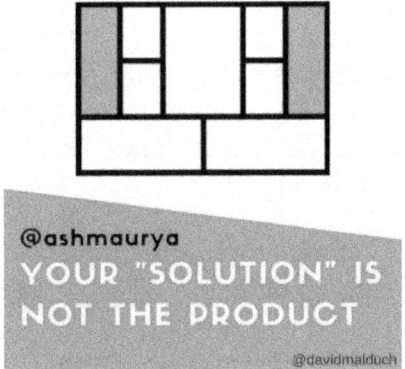

The rest is nothing but text that doesn't add value, it's about going from an Summary thinking of you and what you want, to an Summary thought in how I can help, what we're capable of doing for others, what can we solve.

Of course, it goes without saying, based on the absolute truth.

In the long summary part you can explain more about yourself, your qualities, skills, etc.

5.6.3 How to Plan and Manage our Summary

As you can see, the summary's creation won't be something that you'll pull off in 5 minutes and remains unchanged forever. Instead, it'll continually evolve.

If you're thinking "I'm going to do a definitive one, and when I have it, I'll put it up", big mistake. You'd go months or years without a summary and, what's worse, losing opportunities.

Have a more natural approach to it, let's plant a seed, and let's make our version 1.0 of the summary, which will continually grow, improving its quality and effectiveness, but that will come with work done during time. That's how plants grow.

Since we'll continually be modifying the summary, every time you change it, LinkedIn only saves the last version. To keep a history of all the changes we've done, and to keep all the versions we've written, in case we want to recover a phrase we wrote, you can create a Word document and save each version of the Summary you do in it.

In my case, I prefer to use Evernote (it's free), if you don't have it, you can sign up here http://ow.ly/3x4J30cNwJB

Inside Evernote, I've created a Note called "LinkedIn Summary English", and I follow this structure in it:

Note Title: LinkedIn Summary English

Content:

2018-03-02

Text, text text text text text text text text text text text text text text text text text text text text text text text text text text text text text text text text text text text.

2017-06-01

Text, text text text text text text text text text text text text text text text text text text text text text text text text text text text text text text text text text text.

2016-05-12

Text, text text text text text text text text text text text text text text text text text text text text text text text text.

In the title, as you'll see, I write the name of the language, because further on we'll see how to do the profile in other languages.

If I create a new version of the profile on 2018, above the "2017-06-01" I create a new line, example "2018-03-02" and below it I put the new text, I always put the latest version on top of everything, so when I enter, I see what the latest version is and I don't have to go all the way down.

The format I use for dates is YYYY-MM-DD (year, month, and day). Here I show you how I do it; now you need to adapt it to your way of working.

5.6.4 Designing our Summary

5.6.4.1 Techniques for Designing it

As a help to face the creation of your Summary and its improvement, both if you still don't have one as in case you already have one, we're going to use the Elevator pitch technique [7], which I'll explain now.

This exercise is about creating a clear, simple, and direct message where you're capable, in a quiet and paused way, of explaining what really interests you, and doing it in around 60 seconds.

---

[7] Wiki https://en.wikipedia.org/wiki/Elevator_pitch

The exercise is that you find yourself with the person you wished to contact (future client, recruiter, etc.), you meet them when you enter the elevator, and the both of you enter alone, he pushes the 6th floor button, and you have all that time to speak to them and, specially, generating interest.

Next, I'll show you a video training by Chris Westfall "The Art of the Elevator Pitch". I recommend you see it, so you get familiar with this technique.

https://www.youtube.com/watch?v=GqsWKaR9Q6M

Another video you can see is a fragment of the movie "The Pursuit of Happiness" where Will Smith does his Elevator pitch. You can see it here.

https://www.youtube.com/watch?v=gHXKitKAT1E

As an extra, here's an interview conducted to the man who inspired the movie "The Pursuit of Happiness" where he speaks about the "secret of success".

https://www.youtube.com/watch?v=wTOk2OgxobY

5.6.4.2 Steps to Create our Summary:

1. **What audience are you trying to reach?**

    Here, things like "everyone" or "everything" won't do. We can't create a message that works for everyone; youths, adults, men, women, unemployed, professionals, directors, businessmen, etc.

    The more specific we are, the more effective we'll be.

    Who's the user of your product/service? What problem or necessity are we going to fulfill? How are we going to do it?

    How urgent is that problem? The more urgent it is (we're in the desert and we're the only ones with a water vending machine), the easier the sale will be.

2. **About you, how you bring value, generating trust.**

    Who are you and what's your experience.

    Why are you capable of achieving the success (solution) you're explaining? Have you achieved it before? Can you explain some successful cases?

    Prove to me I can trust you.

3. **Why they should pick you.**

    ¿How are you different from the others? Why should it be you the person they must contact?

    Specially, it can't be an item list, it has to be a text that is natural and easy to read.

5.6.4.3 Length of the Text

Less is more

Since we have the possibility of making a long summary and then creating the top two lines, we'll start by creating the long one, which is always easier. And once we have it, we'll make the summary on the two lines on top of everything. To create this text, follow the points we just saw, think from the client's point of view, so they can exactly understand what you can do for them, what value you bring.

If your situation is job hunting, it's not about what you've studied or what you can do generally, instead, it's about what you're going to do for the company if they hire you, what are you capable of, and specially what you can prove you've been able to do, which responsibilities you've assumed/had, have you been in charge of people? Have you managed teams? Have you lead projects? Which initiatives have you lead? Which improvements have you done in your job position/company? What are you really an expert in? Can we give examples (no need to name the client) of cases with figures? X Volume of sales, growth of x%. Always as long as it can be proved. Remember to summarize.

Introducing techniques like Storytelling[8] is also a good idea, but that's when you have the summary done and you want to do a more advanced and powerful one. In the long text, am I interested in indicating or which brands you are/have been a representative/distributor? Do you want to be located for some techniques/specialties that you know or perform? You can put that inside texts at the end of the summary, so you can also participate in the searches and appear on the results.

---

[8] https://en.wikipedia.org/wiki/Storytelling

Chapter 5: Profile – Contact Card   85

5.6.4.4 Writing the Text

In order to write our summary, we go to our LinkedIn profile and we click on the pencil on the top right section.

After we click the pencil, this screen will show up, and if we go to the end we'll see the field "Summary".

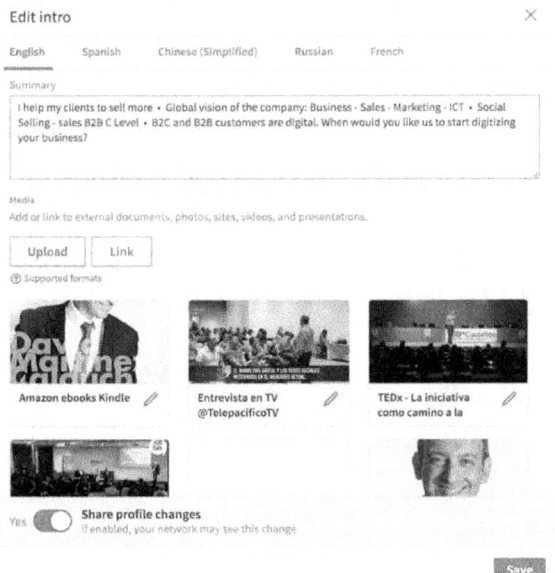

That field is where you have to write the Summary. Once you have it, we click on Save and you'll see two lines where it cuts look, you'll have to check in on a Smartphone, since it's cut differently there. So open the LinkedIn app in your Smartphone to check it out.

If the size of the field is too small to write, you can widen it by clicking and dragging the bottom right corner.

> I help my clients to sell more • Global vision of the company: Business - Sales - Marketing - ICT • Social Selling - sales B2B C Level • B2C and B2B customers are digital. When would you like us to start digitizing your business?

And the max size is 2000 characters.

I personally do not recommend you write directly on this field, I'd do it on Word or Evernote, and when you have it, you copy it and paste it here.

As you may have seen, on the image on the previous page, since I have a profile in several languages, the languages appear on the top, to write the summary in each one of them.

> Edit intro   ×
> English   Spanish   Chinese (Simplified)   Russian   French

Further on, we'll see how to create a LinkedIn profile in several languages, but to get to that moment, fist you need to do the profile we're working on right now very well.

Don't rush to go to the next point of the book, atop for a little while and work on the Summary, this is a fundamental piece in your profile and the effectiveness you'll achieve in the actions you perform later in LinkedIn.

Chapter 5: Profile – Contact Card 87

5.6.5 Multimedia Content

5.6.5.1 Functioning

One of the features we already had on the previous profile version, and still remains in this new version, is being able to post multimedia in our summary. These contents appear at the end of the whole summary.

The changes in this new version are 2. In the previous version, the content appeared as a gallery, one below the other, and now you can see that only 3 are visible, and there are arrows in the top right section to see the rest. And the other change is that, in the previous version, you could see all the multimedia content by default when you entered the Profile and, in our current case, if you don't click the "See more" button, you can't reach that multimedia content.

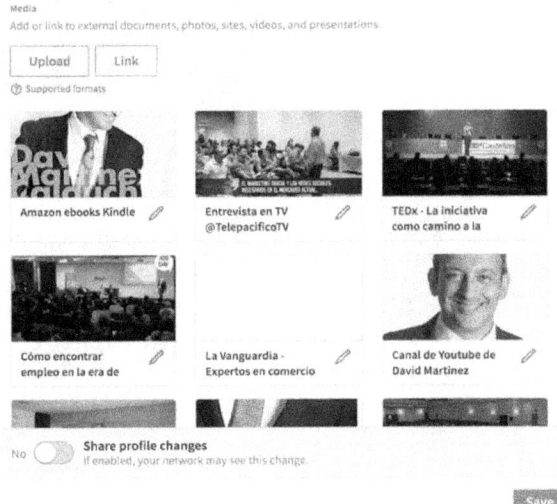

Right below the Summary is where we have the buttons to add our multimedia content.

Media
Add or link to external documents, photos, sites, videos, and presentations.

Upload   Link

You can link any content with a URL (Link button) or directly upload the content to LinkedIn. The supported formats are:

- Presentations: .pdf, .ppt, .pps, .pptx, .ppsx, .pot, .potx, .odp

- Documents: .pdf, .doc, .docx, .rtf, .odt

- Images: .png, .jpg, .jpeg

In this website you have all the admitted contents you can through a "Link" URL http://embed.ly/providers

The objective is including a more visual and engaging content, including audiovisual, which will make the person who reached this section interact with the content and stay in the profile for longer.

Chapter 5: Profile – Contact Card 89

You can include content where you or your company appear (press, awards, etc.), the catalog of products/services, your company's presentation (PowerPoint, Prize –via URL-), a YouTube video, etc.

Examples of works, interviews, radio programs where you've participated, a link to you work gallery, etc.

5.6.5.2 Adding Content

Let's go through how to include content step by step. In my case, I'm going to use my Amazon writer account.

https://www.amazon.com/author/davidmcalduch

This screen appears, I click on the book "Social Selling" and I copy the address, in this case http://amzn.to/2tygeV2

Now we go to LinkedIn, on the top right corner of the screen, we click on "Me", a menu rolls out and we click on "View Profile"

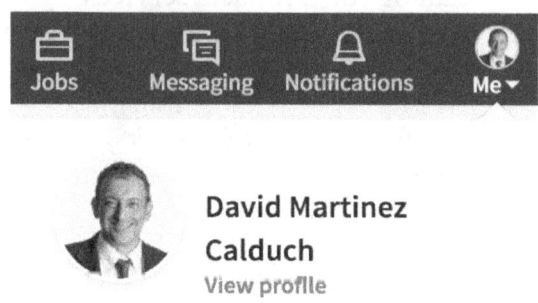

We're in our profile now, we click the pencil button to modify the Summary.

We go to the end of the Summary and, under "Media", we click the "Link" button and we paste the URL we have.

| Paste or type a link to a file or video | Add |

After pasting it, we click "Add". LinkedIn will find the content and load the title and description, both can be modified if you wish.

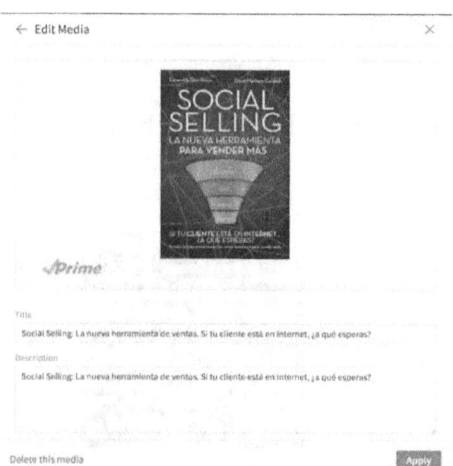

Chapter 5: Profile – Contact Card

We click "Apply" when we're done and we'll have it published in our Summary, as you can see below.

5.6.5.3 Eliminating Multimedia Content

To erase content that you no longer want to appear on your summary, follow these steps:

1. Enter your LinkedIn profile
2. Click the pencil to edit the Summary
3. Go to the end of the Media zone
4. Click on the content pencil
5. When you're inside the content, click on "Delete this media"

Delete this media Apply

5.6.6 Creation of Contents

In the Summary, enter the option of uploading content directly and linking them. I personally prefer the second option, and I'll explain why. It's way more laborious, but in the long run it generates way more positioning and results.

Let's see this work structure:

1. We create a presentation for our company (PowerPoint, Keynote, Canva.com)
2. We convert it to PDF
3. We create an account on Slideshare.net (LinkedIn's property) using our own LinkedIn account.
4. We upload the file
5. Slideshare will give us a URL we can now link with the "Link" button.

I imagine you'll be wondering why you should circle around so much, if you can just upload the PDF directly with the "Upload" button in your Summary, and it'll look the same in the end.

And here's the key: now you have it in your profile, where you wanted it, but you also have it on Slideshare. If you don't know Slideshare, I'll explain it to you, so you understand its potential. YouTube is *the* video channel, and Slideshare is the same for Presentations and PDFs, which will help you diffuse your presentation, apart from your LinkedIn Profile.

Slideshare has over 80 million professionals, with more than 18 million contents posted in 40 categories, and it's among the 100 most visited websites in the world.

Of course, you can directly upload the PDF to LinkedIn but, don't you believe you'll lose diffusion and SEO by not posting it on Slideshare? I can confirm, yes, you'll lose a LOT of opportunities.

Chapter 5: Profile – Contact Card

And the same thing happens with other types of contents. Imagine we do a video, I'd create a YouTube channel and upload the video and, from there, I'd link the video to the Summary with the "Link" button.

YouTube is the second largest search engine in the world, and the third most visited website behind Google and Facebook.[9]

If you want to upload pictures, I'd post them on Flickr (property of Yahoo!), then I'd create an album, and would post the Album's link to the Summary.

Let's see my Flickr (company) account, we signed up on 2010 and went to the paid version on 2012.

https://www.flickr.com/photos/solucionafacil/

---

[9] Source: Brandwatch

![statistics showing Fotos 92,810 | Galería 2,174 | Álbumes 7,935 | Colecciones 0 | Galerías 4 | Total 102,923]

We already have a total of 102.923 visits to our photos in Flickr, therefore Flickr is helping us with the diffusion of our contents, in this case our photos. The company's name appears in all of them and if you click that name, the website, telephone, etc. appear.

To summarize, I want you to understand that, if we post the contents in these and other platforms, and link them to LinkedIn, the content is visible both in your LinkedIn profile, and these platforms also have a radio of diffusion among their users and diffuse our contents for us.

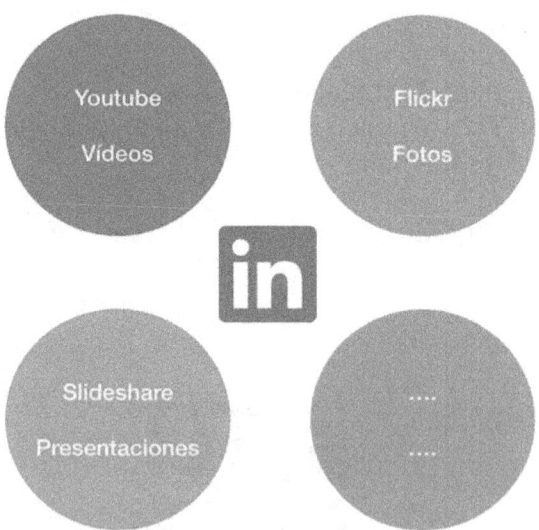

And to create Presentations, Infographics, Product Sheets, Magazines, Catalogs, etc. you can use www.canva.com, of which we'll give you an example on how to do it later.

Chapter 6

Profile – Activity and Results

After the initial sheet we've seen, what comes next is a summary of our activity and the results we've achieved.

This first part is only visible for you.

And this is visible for anyone who visits your profile.

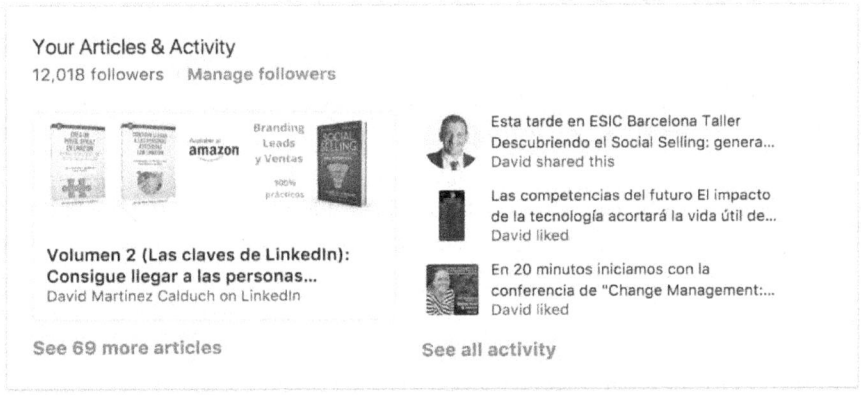

6.1 Statistics of our Actions

LinkedIn offers a great variety of statistics with which we can see our evolution, starting from the changes we make in our profile, the posts we make, and our interactions with other professionals.

Now let's see which data it grants us, and how this data look in the free version and the Premium (paid) version.

These are the data shown about the performance I'm having with my profile, let's see the data from left to right and analyze what they mean.

6.2 Visits to your Profile

This information is very important because they're either people who know you and have typed your full name to locate you, or people looking for a term (word they've entered in the search bar, a technology, knowledge, brand, service, product, profession, etc.) and you've appeared on the results and, from there, they've entered to see your profile.

With this, we've at least achieved that they see our contact sheet and our Elevator pitch.

If we click on the number of visits to our profile (right now don't worry about the number that appears), the important thing is seeing the number we have now and increase it over time.

Chapter 6: LinkedIn Profile

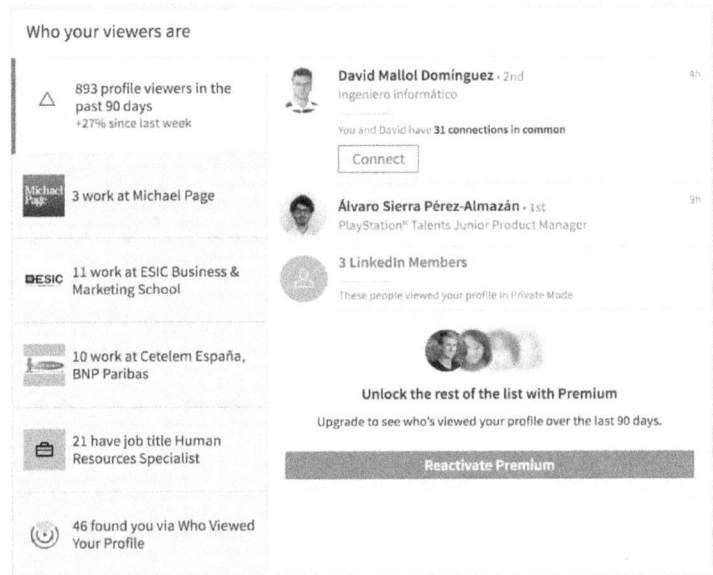

When we enter the statistics screen, it indicates us that the figure of 893 visits corresponds to the last 90 days. 90 days are 12 weeks, so 893/12 = 74. That indicates me I've had a 27% growth this week over the past week.

We can conclude I've achieved that 74 people come to my profile every week to find out who I am, what I do, etc. This can be focused towards generating Leads, job searching, etc.

In the left part we can see that it indicates several companies, of which several people have come to see my profile, and below everything we have 21 HR people, and at the end, 46 people I had visited and they had visited me. This whole left section changes depending on the results.

By clicking in any of the options on the left, they people that have visited us appear on the right side. On the upper image you'll see that only 3 are shown, since this is the free version and it only shows visits in the last 7 days.

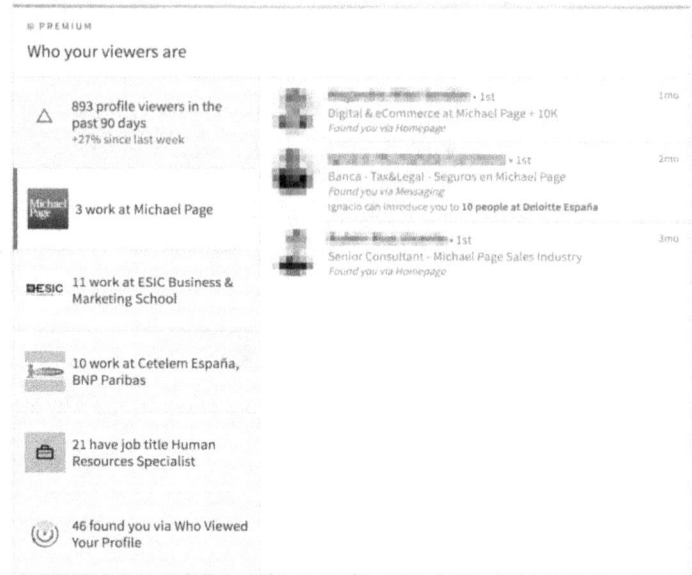

And with the Premium version (any of them) we can now see all the people that have visited us in the last 90 days and, in the upper image, you can see the three people from Michael Page that have visited my profile.

6.3 Posts Visualizations

In this case, this is the information that LinkedIn shows in the middle, and we'll analyze it, but these data in the center and the right will change depending on the information LinkedIn deems more important to show you.

It indicates us that among our post feed, there's a post that has 8,935 people who've seen it. We click on the figure to see more information, and it'll take us to the following screen.

Chapter 6: LinkedIn Profile

In the part below the post we see the interaction the post has had (likes and comments, which make this post be seen by level 1 contacts of the person who interacting, in other words, our level 2) and how many people have seen it.

If we click on the icon with the graphic (with the arrow), or the number 10,231 we'll go to the statistics screen.

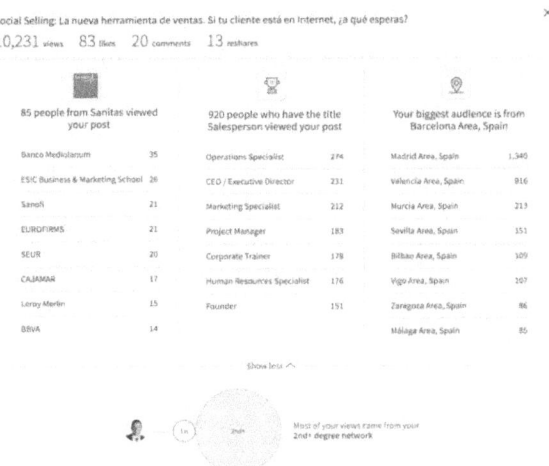

On the top section we see that it indicates the total of visualizations, likes, comments, and times shared.

After that it tells us from more to less, the amount of people of each company that have seen it. In the central section it's shown by position: 920 salespersons, 231 CEOs, 212 Marketing specialists, 176 HR, etc. And, in the last one, by posts.

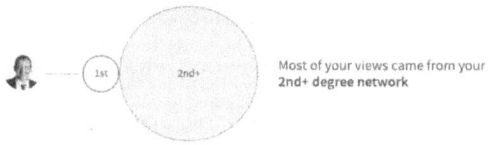

At the end you can see that it indicates us this post has skipped my level 1 contacts and that, specially, the great majority of people that are seeing it are people that aren't my direct contacts, and that's why the 2nd+ circle is way bigger than the 1st.

What you can't find out or see, is which people they are concretely, LinkedIn won't give you that list.

The first option, "Articles" corresponds to the posts we do with LinkedIn's article writing platform called Pulse, where you also have access to your post's statistics.

And on the third option, the things from the other two options appear, plus every content we've Liked, shared, or participated in the comments section.

Chapter 6: LinkedIn Profile 101

6.4 Search Appearances

★ 893 Who's viewed your profile	8,935 Views of your post in the feed	3,667 Weekly search appearances

The last value is a new statistic that LinkedIn has incorporated, which is very interesting. It informs us of the times we've appeared in searches conducted by other people.

In my concrete case, it indicates I've appeared 3,667 times every week in search results.

If we click the number, we'll go to the screen where the information is expanded.

Weekly search stats

3667

number of times your profile appeared in search results between June 13 - June 20

Where your searchers work	Number of searches
IEM BUSINESS SCHOOL Higher Education 11-50 employees	229
Hays Staffing and Recruiting 5,001-10,000 employees	26
ESIC Business & Marketing School Education Management 201-500 employees	24
51-200 employees	20
Biotechnology 201-500 employees	18

Chapter 6: LinkedIn Profile

And further down it tells us which positions the people conducting the searches where we have appeared have.

6.5 Articles and Activity Box

This box contains part of the information we've already seen, but we have it in a quick view form, so we don't have to go through a longer road.

Chapter 7

Slideshare

80% of the traffic that reaches Slideshare to see its contents comes from search engines.

Due to the importance of content creation and the power that Slideshare has, in this chapter we're going to learn how to sign up on Slideshare, how to set it up, and how to post content. From there, you can link it with the sections of your profile.

7.1 Signing up on Slideshare

To sign up on Slideshare we go to their website:

https://www.slideshare.net

On the top right corner, you can see the "Signup" button.

If you want to change Slideshare's language first, in the bottom of the website you can select one of the following languages.

English   Español   Português   Français   Deutsch

When you click "Signup", this screen will appear.

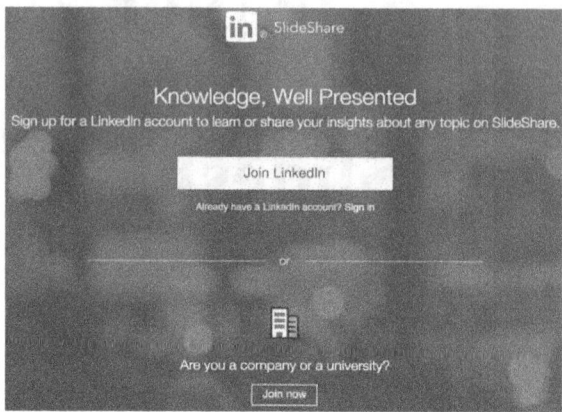

We have two options. For us, it's the "Sign in" button, and we sign up using our LinkedIn profile.

If what we want is to create a Slideshare account for our company or university (only if you have the entity's express permission to sign up), then you must click the button below "Join Now".

We'll click on "Sign in".

And we click "Login with LinkedIn", where they'll ask for our email and password we used to register on LinkedIn, that that's how both accounts are linked, LinkedIn and Slideshare.

7.2 Account Configuration

The first thing we're going to do is configuring our Slideshare account, so our info appears.

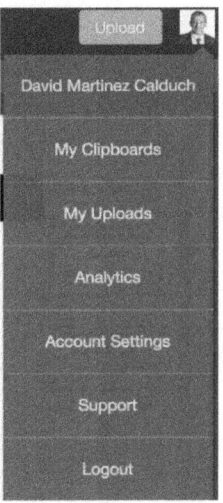

On the top right corner of the screen, your LinkedIn Profile picture will appear (or the image of a grey person if you still haven't set it up), click the photo so the menu rolls out and select "Account Settings".

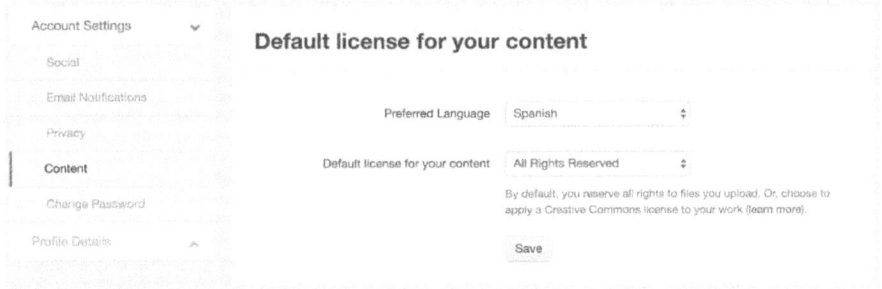

On the screen that appears, on the left part we have a menu, and within "Account Settings", we select the option "Content", and a screen will appear on the right side where we'll indicate the language in which we'll upload the content and which type of copyright we want to apply.

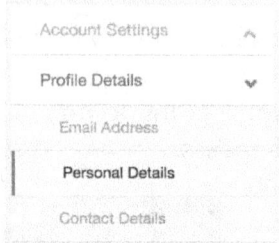

Now, on the left menu we select the last option, "Profile Details" and within it we select "Personal Details", and this screen will appear.

What you have to do here is to fill every field. If you don't have a website, you'll see how to put the address of your LinkedIn profile later.

Chapter 7: Slideshare   **109**

To upload the photography, modify it from a computer to adapt it to the size requested by Slideshare.

The size must be 96x96px

The admitted formats are jpg, png or gif

The file's maximum size is 500KB

The objective is that every time you post content, it's linked to your data and, from there, people have the possibility of visiting your LinkedIn profile to have more information about you.

Use the same photo you have in LinkedIn.

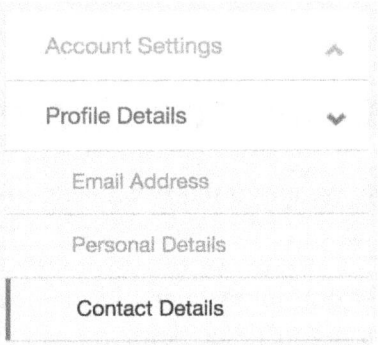

Then we'll go to the last option in the menu, "Contact Details", where we'll see the screen you'll see below. We must fill the fields we deem useful for people to locate us.

Now we've signed up and we've configured all the necessary data to have our complete sheet in Slideshare, and now we can start creating our first content.

7.3 Creating our Content

Let's see how we can quickly create content in Canva.com

Let's go to www.canva.com (in a computer), up in the right part we click this button so every kind of content we can create pops out, the button you'll see below:

Within the "Documents" category, we have "Presentation"

Chapter 7: Slideshare

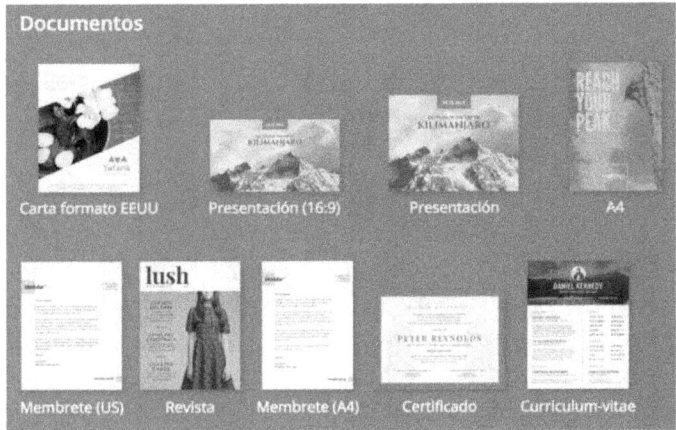

By clicking on the Presentation, a new window opens. In the left part of the screen we already have the created designs, now we only have to select which one adapts better to your corporate image, or the type of content you wish to share.

These are some samples of the designs.

By placing the cursor above each of the designs, you'll see that it'll indicate a number right on the top right corner, it's the amount of different slides that are already designed inside.

And by clicking on the design we've chosen, it'll drop down and inform us for which kind of contents these slides are created.

And below, it'll show us the design of the 10 slides of this model.

Chapter 7: Slideshare

The same thing can be done with the rest of the designs until you find the one you like the most.

For this example, I'll use this one. If it's the first time you use Canva.com, I recommend you use the same one I'm showing you, so it's easier for you.

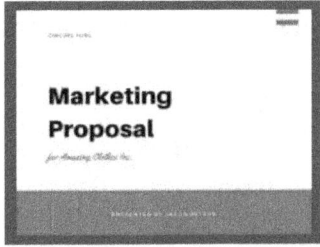

In the gallery of the 10 slides, we click on the first one, and it'll appear on the center of the screen, our first pre-designed slide.

Now we'll click on the texts, and change them for texts we want to appear, we can change the type of font, color, etc. With the changes I do, it ends up like this.

By clicking on the text, this toolbar will appear on the upper part, where you can change the type of font, size, color, etc.

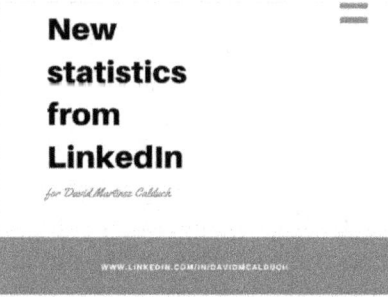

Below this slide we have the button to add another new slide.

By clicking it, the slide 2 in blank will appear, and on the left side (where the 10 pre-designed slides are), we select which type of design we want for the second one. For the second one, I'll select this one.

I modify it, so my info appears. No, on the left side of the screen we click on "Uploaded Files".

Chapter 7: Slideshare

We click the "" button to upload a picture of ourselves that we have on our computer.

By clicking on the image, you can change its size, turn it around, etc.

And the design of my second slide ends up like this.

Now, again, we click the button "Add a new page", to create the third slide, and again we select the slide design that better adapts to the content we're about to post from the left side.

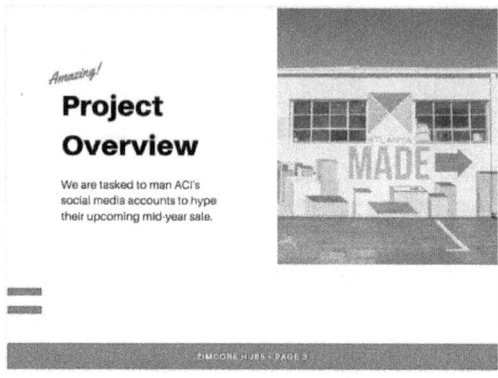

I change the colors and the texts, I click the image and delete it, and I add the images I have prepared. This is the result.

On the right side, you'll see it indicates we are on the 3rd slide, and there's a two sheets icon, click that two sheets icon, and it'll copy the slide, since the next one is going to be very similar.

Chapter 7: Slideshare

Once this slide is done, we copy it again to make the next one.

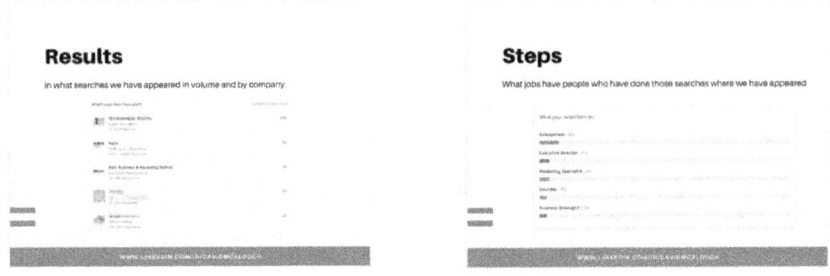

And we repeat it two more times to finish putting the rest of the content.

We copy the last one again, and we make a conclusions slide.

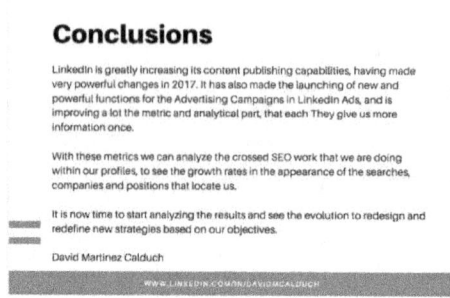

We click on the top of the screen to set the title we want the PDF to have when we download it.

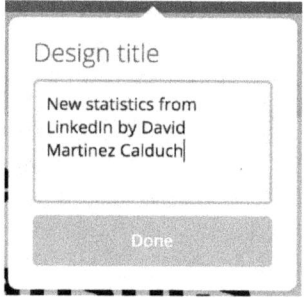

And on the top right part, we click the download button. I've selected "Standard PDF".

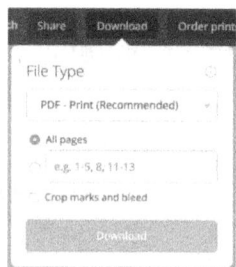

Now, there are only 2 steps left, posting the PDF in Slideshare and adding it to our LinkedIn profile, or posting it to our wall.

Chapter 7: Slideshare   119

7.4 Uploading Content

We go to the www.Slideshare.net website, and on the top right corner we have the "Upload" button.

This screen will appear. We take the PDF we've downloaded to our computer and we drop it in the middle of this box.

Now you have to fill every field and click "Publish".

The moment when the presentation is already published (I'll take very little time), it'll take us to the page, so we can see it, and up on the browser bar we have our presentation's URL. In my case, this is it:

https://www.slideshare.net/davidmcalduch/new-statistics-from-linked-in-by-david-martinez-calduch

With this URL, we can now add this presentation to our media section of our Summary, in our LinkedIn profile.

7.5 Publishing Content

To make another example, what I'm going to do in this case, is publishing this content we've created on my LinkedIn wall. Let's see how to do it.

I go to LinkedIn's homepage, clicking the blue In icon on the top left, or the house icon up on the menu. You'll see this box on the top center part of the screen.

We click where it says, "Share an article, photo, or update" and paste the URL for our Slideshare presentation.

Chapter 7: Slideshare

LinkedIn loads the content and gives us the revisualization. Now the written UR is no longer necessary, so we delete it and we can write the text we deem appropriate to achieve the most impact possible and attracting more views.

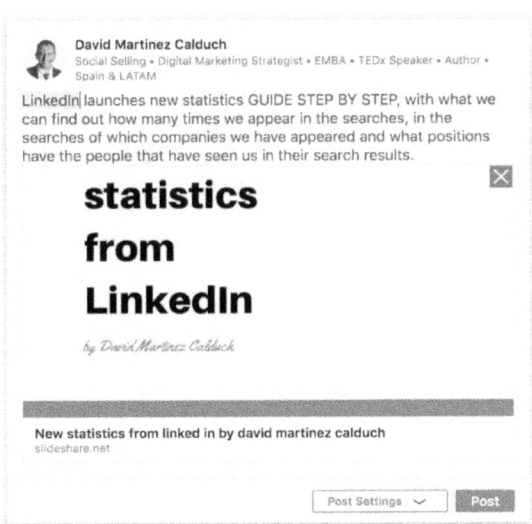

Now we only need to click the "Post" button to publish. The first time you do the creating content process, it'll be a little slower, but with practice you'll see it's quick and easy to do.

Next, we'll see the evolution of the real visualizations of this publication and it's % of growth.

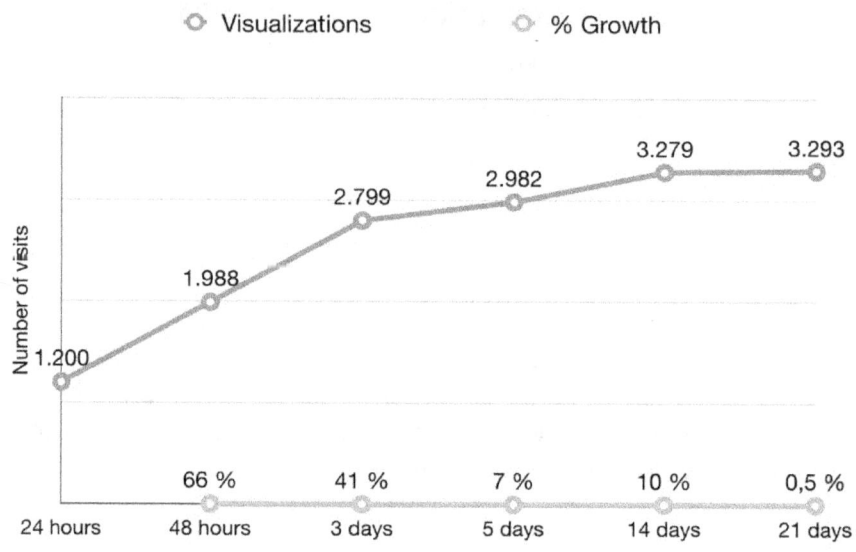

Chapter 8

Profile – Contact Information

On the left part, if we're on the desktop version, there's a zone where we can enter more information about ourselves.

8.1 Structure and Functioning

On the profile's upper section, in the right zone, we have "Contact and Personal Info".

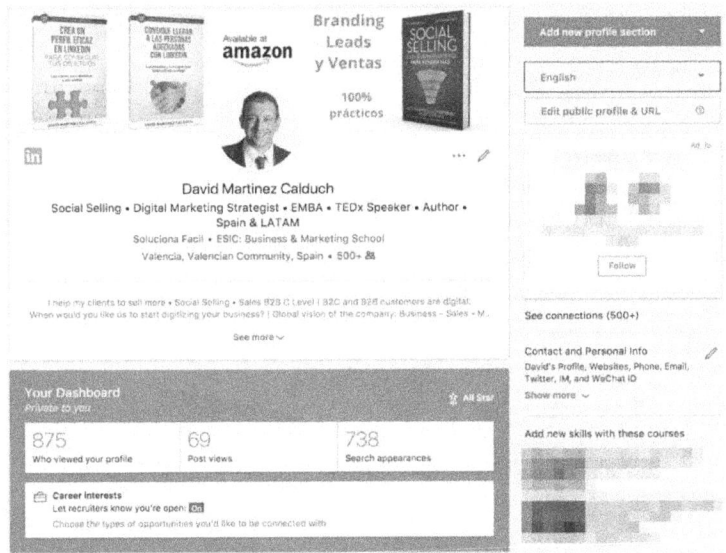

By clicking on "Show more" this screen appears.

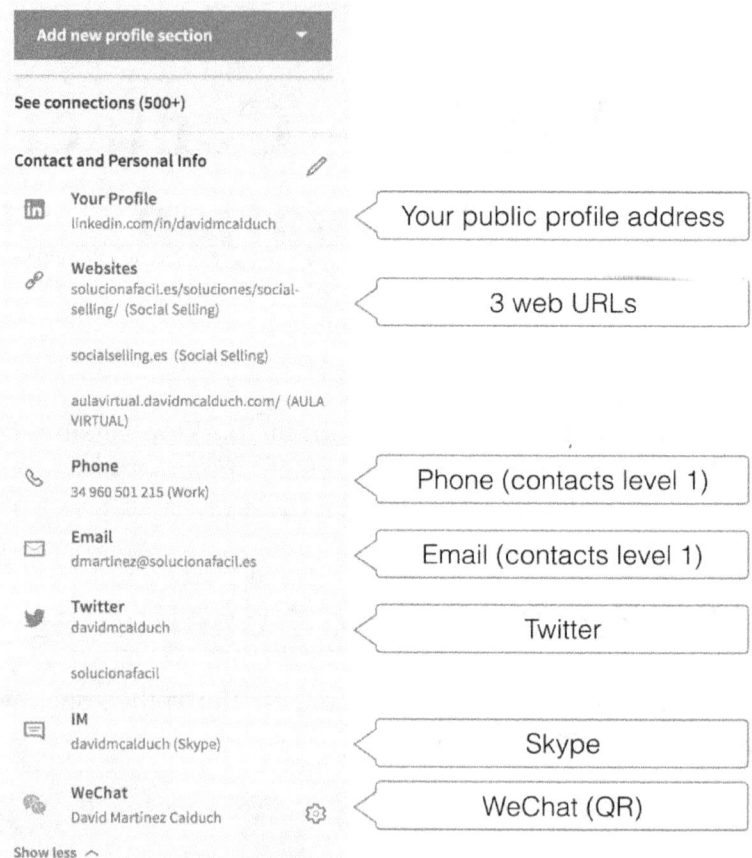

To be able to modify the info that appears, we click on the blue pencil on top of everything, next to "Contact and Personal Info", and the screen we'll see below will appear.

Chapter 8: Profile – Contact Information

Edit contact info

Profile URL
linkedin.com/in/davidmcalduch ↗

Website URL
| solucionafacil.es/soluciones/social-selling/ | Other |

Type (Other)
Social Selling

Remove website

Website URL
| socialselling.es | Other |

Type (Other)
Social Selling

Remove website

Website URL
| aulavirtual.davidmcalduch.com/ | Other |

Type (Other)
AULA VIRTUAL

Remove website

Phone
| 34 960 501 215 | Work |

No ⬤ **Share profile changes**
If enabled, your network may see this change.

Save

Now we're going to see each one of the fields in order to properly configure them.

8.2 Public Profile Address

The public profile address is very important for improving a LinkedIn profile URL, and to achieve a better position on search engines (Google, Bing, Yahoo!, etc.).

If you still haven't configured your public profile address, it's possible it looks something like this:

linkedin.com/in/davidmcalduch-pub-838eic89e3 (example)

My customized address is

www.linkedin.com/in/davidmcalduch

As you can see, it's much easier on the eyes.

> Profile URL
> linkedin.com/in/davidmcalduch ↗

We click on the address or the arrow and a new window will open.

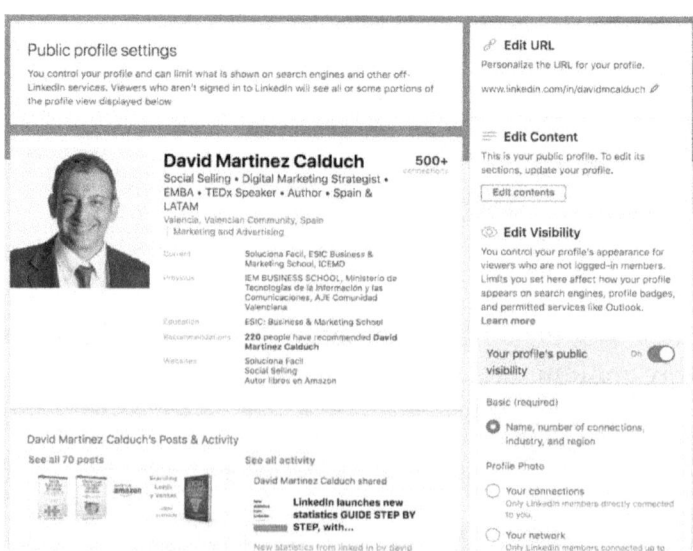

Chapter 8: Profile – Contact Information

Edit public profile URL

Enhance your personal brand by creating a custom URL for your LinkedIn public profile.

www.linkedin.com/in/davidmcalduch

On the top right part, we have this box, and we click on the blue pencil to customize our address.

Edit URL

Personalize the URL for your profile.

www.linkedin.com/in/davidmcalduch

Note: Your custom URL must contain 5-30 letters or numbers. Please do not use spaces, symbols, or special characters.

Cancel **Save**

Now you can customize your public profile address, but you must keep in mind:

- Once you modify it, try not to change it again
- It's a website URL
- You have to write everything together without spaces
- It has to be 5-30 characters long
- You can use special characters (ñ, ç, accents, underscores, etc.)
- You can use dashes - if you want

Once you've written it, click "Save", and if it's not already in use, it'll save. Otherwise, it'll ask you to use another.

On the bottom right part, mark the box "Make my public profile visible to everyone".

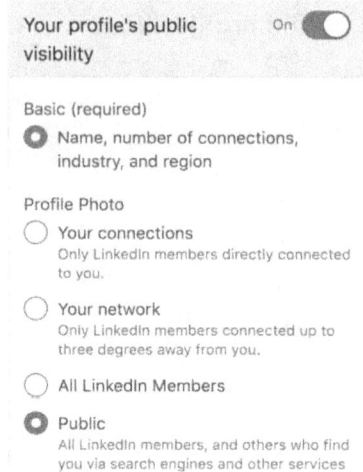

And activate all the boxes you have and click Save. Don't worry if you don't have as many as me. Later, we'll see how to arrange them. Finally, we click the final "Save" button.

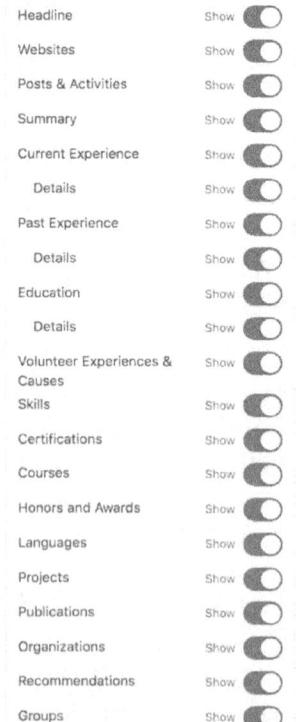

Now you can click this button you have on the upper right, "Back to LinkedIn.com", which will open a new window. Close the other tabs to avoid confusion.

What we just did was telling LinkedIn that we want our profile on the search engines for them to index it so we can appear in their searches, which will get us more visits to our profile. Every time you modify your profile, LinkedIn sends it over again for indexation.

8.3 Analyzing Search Engines' Results

Let's make an example, I'll do it with me. After seeing it, you should do it with yourself to see the results and analyzing them.

https://www.google.com/search?q=david+martinez+calduch&gws_rd=cr&dcr=0&ei=NqGNWqHHEcbzUO--k5gI

As you can see in the results, the first one that appears is my LinkedIn profile, with my public profile address, so you can see the power it has when appearing in search results.

Of course, now we'd have to make searches with your key words and see the results.

This point is extensive to detail, since we enter in a SEO positioning strategy with LinkedIn and other resources, to position yourself not only on your name and last name, but also on your business lines and objectives.

8.4 Websites

Now we're back to our profile, and in contact information we click the pencil again.

 We can include a max of three addresses for our websites, as you can see in the image.

 The objective is that, when people look for more info on you, you can send them to the websites you're interested that they see.

 Websites we can include:

- The website of the company where you work.

- The URL of the website of a specific product or brand of the company's website

- The URL of the website where the company has a launch, a landing page

- Your website / blog
- Your Flickr/500px photo gallery
- Your Instagram photos
- Your Slideshare presentations
- Your YouTube channel
- Your Behance designs
- Your Postcast channel
- Etc.

Basically, you can enter any URL address.

When you introduce the URLs, you'll see on the right side that you have a drop-down list. If you select "Other", a new field appears where you can enter the title you want. Think of your SEO strategy.

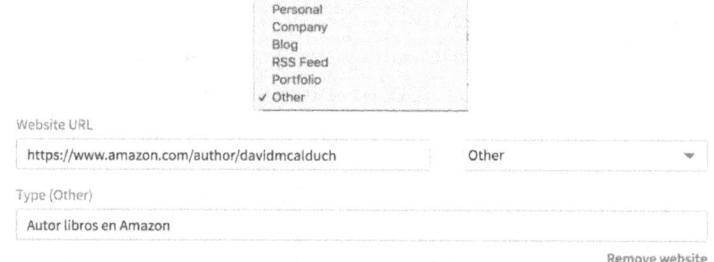

8.5 Telephone and Address

Here you can indicate the telephone you want to be seen. Is it the one in your office? And the address; of course, don't put your home address, this is a Professional Profile. If you must, leave it blank.

Chapter 8: Profile – Contact Information   133

8.6 Email/s

Email address
dmartinez@solucionafacil.es ↗

The next field that appears is the email addresses, with the one you used to register on LinkedIn.

We click on the email or on the blue arrow, and a new tab/window will open. Here's the address to go directly (in a computer).

https://www.linkedin.com/psettings/email

You can only add and keep on the list, those emails that exist and you have access to.

When you enter this screen and perform certain actions, as a security measure, LinkedIn will ask for your LinkedIn password to confirm it's you.

The way LinkedIn confirms you know someone, is because you have the other person's email address, the email they used to sign up on LinkedIn.

And the way for making easier for other people to invite us, is adding all of our emails, so every person who knows us for each one of those emails is able to invite us.

 The only address visible to your level 1 contacts is the one you mark as "Primary".

Add email address

At the center, below everything, you have the box "Add email address" to add more emails to which you have access. When you click on it, this screen will appear.

Introduce the email address and click the "Send verification" button. LinkedIn will send you a verification email. You must enter your email, open it, and click the link to demonstrate you're the owner of the email, and it'll appear on the list.

Here you have an example of the email you'll get.

Chapter 8: Profile – Contact Information 135

If what you want is to remove an email you have registered, when you click "Remove", it'll ask us for our LinkedIn account password as a safety measure.

8.7 Twitter Accounts

We can also include our Twitter accounts.

But in order to add them, we must go to a different screen.

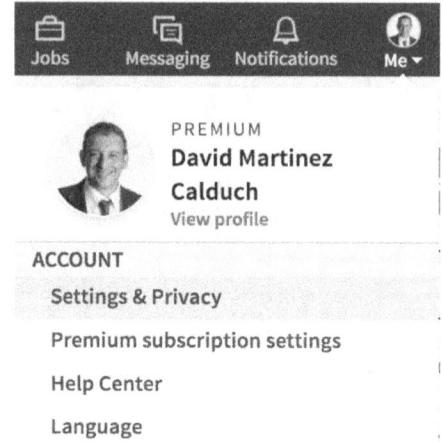

Let's go to the top right menu on "Me", and after dropping the menu down we select "Settings & Privacy", and a new window/tab will open.

We select the upper menu "Account", and we click "Partners and Third Parties" on the bottom left, and on the center we have the option "Twitter Settings", when we click it, the screen we see below will appear, where we can add and remove the Twitter accounts that will appear on our LinkedIn profile.

Chapter 8: Profile – Contact Information

Manage your Twitter Settings

ACCOUNTS

davidmcalduch
[Remove] Everyone ▾

solucionafacil
[Remove] Everyone ▾

Add another Twitter account

SHARING TWEETS

Which Twitter account would you like to share from? solucionafacil ▾

Save changes or Cancel

You'll see that this screen still has the old LinkedIn aspect, so it still has to get a full redesign.

Chapter 9

Profile – Job Positions

The Professional Experience/Job Positions section is key for showing how our professional career has been, what we have done, which achievements we've had, and what we're doing now.

9.1 Junior Profile

In case you're starting your professional career now, it's normal that you put little content in this section, don't worry, it's not a sprint; your professional career is a long-distance race, a marathon.

Plan well what you want to achieve, where you want to get, and work hard, with drive and illusion.

If you've done internships in a company, when you put them in your LinkedIn profile, you need to do this reflection, in the internships I've done, have I developed functions of the position? Have I done the work? Or have they had me make copies or repetitive tasks? Have they been training me? That way, you'll have to focalize that experience.

If you've done internships, as the name indicates, you must name them as such in the position, but there are cases I've known where the person has really developed the position and has made the work assigned to that position. The only difference between those internships and a normal work contract is the type of contract and the salary earned. In those cases, you could value not including the word "internship". This as long as the requirement I'm indicating is fulfilled, and that you may justify it in a clear way.

9.2 Senior Profile

In previous chapters we had already commented which documentation you needed to prepare to work in this section, since over the years we can easily forget the right dates, functions, projects, successes, etc.

In the current work and social situation in which we're living, it's possible you're finding yourself in a career focus shift. You don't have to worry or be overwhelmed, this is the most normal thing in the world, and you'll see how you can reflect that in your profile.

I work with many Managers and Professionals who are doing a shift in their professional careers, and they come to me to see hoy to embody that on their profiles.

Myself, if you check my LinkedIn profile

www.linkedin.com/in/davidmcalduch

You'll see that in 2009 I took a professional shift when I quit my position of IT Chief and opened my own company "Soluciona Facil" where I develop my professional career focused in the world of Sales and Digital Marketing (Social Selling and Digital Marketing Strategies).

Remember that a good professional is such, regardless of the sector and position where they are. So, you professional career path and achievements are key to strengthen your professional profile.

9.3 Structure and Functioning

In the profile's older version, when you visited a profile, every job position was visible. In this new redesign, only the last 5 are shown, and the rest remain hidden.

I'll show you an example at the end of my position as Hootsuite Ambassador and the one which appears fifth, MBA Professor in Target Business School, and as you can see, the blue text "See more positions" appears, and if we click it, the rest of positions are shown.

This also happens in the LinkedIn App.

The objective LinkedIn pursues with this change, is to facilitate the viewing of professional profiles since, in a single glance, you can see the latest things that person has been doing, and if you're interested in going deeper, you can extend it.

9.4 Adding Job Positions

> *Professionals with active job positions receive up to 5 times more connection requests.*
>
> *- LinkedIn*

Now let's see how to create job positions of our professional career.

Here I'll show you one of my job position as example. For you to see an example, let's now register one and see the process step by step.

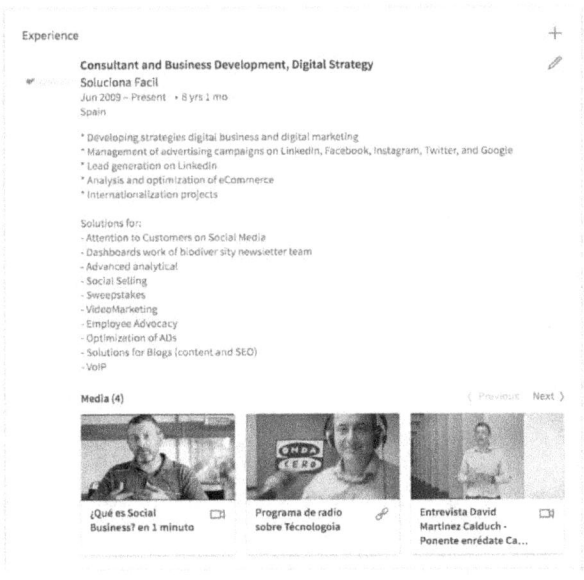

In the Job Positions zone, we click on the blue +, and this screen will appear.

Add experience

English Spanish Chinese (Simplified) Russian French

Title

Company

Location

From
Month
Year

To
Month
Year

I currently work here

Description

Media
Add or link to external documents, photos, sites, videos, and presentations.

Upload Link

Supported formats

No — **Share profile changes**
If enabled, your network may see this change.

Save

Now we're going to check each one of the sections.

If you notice, the last field is if you want to post to your wall that you've modified or added that position, for your level 1 contacts to know.

9.4.1 Position

Title

The first field is the title of your job position, we've seen in the op section of the profile, the "Professional Title", when we saw it, I recommended the creation of a title focused in your objectives, and for you to be a little creative (nothing but the truth).

This point is different to the Professional Title, here you must put:

- The position on your presentation cards
- The position on your contract
- Your real position confirmed by the company

It may happen, and I say so because I know of cases, that the position's "title" isn't very clear. When in doubt, you can check with your company.

9.4.2 Company

The next field we must introduce is the name of the company. Here are a few factors you must keep into account. As you can see in the image below, when you write the company name, it's possible the company shows up. If it does, you have to click the name of the company.

Company
Soluciona Facil
Soluciona Facil
Marketing and Advertising

If the company exists and appears on the list, we must click on it in order to link ourselves and appear as an employee or ex-employee.

All this information will be used by LinkedIn to help us achieve our objectives.

If the company where you work doesn't exist:

- Don't consider registering the company in any case if you don't have the company's express permission, since, if you don't, you'd be committing identity theft.

- Communicate to your company that it's important to have a company profile in LinkedIn, and that, if they deem it timely, they should create it.

If the company where you used to work doesn't exist:

- Imagine that this company has even stopped existing, are you its legal representative? If the answer is no, you can't create it.

- Is it a company where you worked in and exists? Most you can do is contact them so they register it.

9.4.3 Location

> *Over 30% of recruiters use the location when searching for candidates.*
>
> *- LinkedIn*

Location
Region (ex: London, United Kingdom)

In this field, we indicate the place where we develop our job position. If you check my profile as example

www.linkedincom/in/davidmcalduch

You'll see I have positions with different locations: Valencia (Spain), Peru, Colombia, Guatemala, etc.

Location
Valencia
- Valencia Area, Spain
- Valencia, Spain

As you can see in this example, when you type the city, it gives you other options for you to select.

This field is free and isn't locked to what appears on the list. Instead, you can type whatever you want. The list that appears is to help you.

9.4.4 Time Period

Now we have to indicate from which month and year, to which month and year we've been working in that job position. There's no need to include the day.

If this is a current position, you must activate the button you have on the left side, "I currently work here".

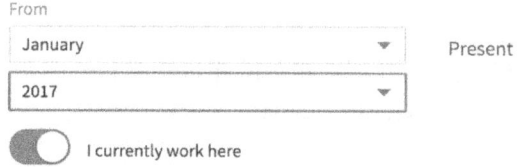

When you do it, the "To" dates disappear, and it shows the word "Present".

But another important change we must be aware us is produced, which we'll see next.

By default, by stating this is our current position, LinkedIn, with the objective of helping us, will change our "Headline", "Professional Title" from above the whole profile, for the combination of our "New Position" + "The Name of the Company", as you can see in the example.

If you notice, below the box, in grey, it indicates you currently have another text set. If you don't want to change what you have now in your "Headline", you have to deactivate the "Update my headline" box.

9.4.5 Description

> *40% of professionals admit it's hard to describe their job position.*
>
> *- LinkedIn*

This is the field where we have to explain what we've done in our job position.

Make one introductory paragraph explaining your position, and then, remember that an excessive text size will make people not read it. We'll be among the other 60% ;-)

 Be brief, concise, think of what you want to transmit, which objective you pursue, and think of the SEO.

 Which functions have you really performed? Even those which don't belong to your position, but you've done them by will.

Which were your main functions? Which initiatives have you lead? Which responsibilities have you assumed?

Have you managed teams? How many and in which tasks/projects/responsibilities?

Have you gotten achievements and

successes? Which? (If they can be counted. If not, don't put them*)

Did you mark any objectives to achieve? What did you achieve?

Has your work been done in a regional, national, or international level? How have you added value to the company from your position?

Can you name which brands/firms you represent? Can you name clients? It's possible you need to ask your company and even your clients for permission to name them.

*If what you're going to put can harm you or your company, don't put it. For example, names of clients, business figures, new lines of products, etc. I have projects with multinational companies whose names I can't include, because the client wants anonymity.

9.4.6 Media

The multimedia contents part works the same as the summary, so let's take this point as learn, in how to incorporate contents.

Remember that in the same way that happens with the summary, only 3 contents are seen, and the rest works as a carousel.

Chapter 9: Job Positions 151

9.4.7 Diffusion and Saving

The only thing left, is deciding if you want to post this position you've added, and you can click the Save button.

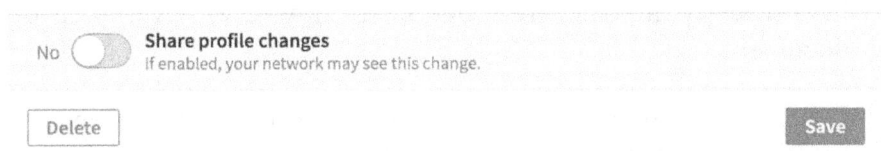

Of course, following your CV, now you have to add the job positions you have in your professional career. My advice is for you to not be in an excessive rush to put a new job position. Evaluate when you consider is the best time for you and your particular case. When well used, the moment you post an update can help you give it more diffusion.

9.5 Rearranging Job Positions

When putting the cursor over a job position, on the right side of the position, these three buttons will appear.

The third button (the blue lines), is for rearranging the job positions, to sort them in the order you prefer.

You can only sort the job positions that are open, that means, those in which you currently work. You can't rearrange those you've closed (stopped working), they're automatically arranged by date.

9.6 Deleting Job Positions

It's possible you may want to delete a job position, this can be done in any time, but remember you can't undo it. Before deleting it, I'd copy all the information to my CV, Evernote, or a document.

The only thing you need to do, is going to the job position, and clicking the blue pencil to indicate you want to modify it.

Right at the end of the position, in the bottom left, you have the "Delete" button.

Chapter 10

Profile – Education

The regulated studies we've performed are very important for our career. In this section we must only include University Degrees, Postgraduate Studies, and Masters. To include courses, you must do so in a section we'll be seeing later.

10.1 Registering Studies

Education

ESIC: Business & Marketing School
ESIC Executive MBA, Máster en Administración y Dirección de Empresas (EMBA)
2016 – 2017

When we click the blue plus sign, this screen will appear.

Edit education

English   Spanish   Chinese (Simplified)   Russian   French

School
ESIC: Business & Marketing School

Degree
Executive MBA

Field of study
Máster en Administración y Dirección de Empresas (EMBA)

Grade

Activities and societies

Ex: Alpha Phi Omega, Marching Band, Volleyball

Time period
From Year   To Year (or expected)
2016   2017

Description

Media
Add or link to external documents, photos, sites, videos, and presentations.

Upload   Link

Supported formats

No — **Share profile changes**
If enabled, your network may see this change.

Delete   Save

Now we'll review each one of the fields, and we'll see what we have to write.

Chapter 10: Education

10.1.1 University

> School
>
> ▪ ESIC: Business & Marketing School
>
> ▪ ESIC: Business & Marketing School
> Madrid Area, Spain

In the same way as when we entered the name of the company, we selected it from the list, here we must also do so with the university. It's very important to click on our university in the list, to link ourselves as Graduates. When we conduct searches, this will help us.

10.1.2 Degree

Type the title of your studies, and a list will appear, you select it, or you can also customize it.

> Degree
>
> Master of Business Administration - MBA
>
> Master of Business Administration - MBA

You must type the official title the University has for it, in my case, I'll leave it as is.

> Degree
>
> Master of Business Administration - MBA Executive

10.1.3 Study Field

In this field we're going to enter the field of our studies. In the same way as the previous field, a list will appear and we'll select the correct one.

> Field of study
>
> Business Administration and Management, General
>
> Business Administration and Management, General

10.1.4 Grade

Here you can include the grade you got, if you consider it relevant.

> Grade
> [   ]

10.1.5 Activities and Societies

In this field you can indicate in which activities you've participated, which have you led, and in which associations and societies have you been.

> Activities and societies
> [   ]
> Ex: Alpha Phi Omega, Marching Band, Volleyball

10.1.6 Time Period

All of this being regulated training, time periods are only specified with the beginning and ending years.

> Time period
> From Year   To Year (or expected)
> [2016   ▼]   [2017   ▼]

10.1.7 Description

Here you can detail any other thing you consider important and that didn't fit the previous fields.

> Description
> [   ]

10.1.8 Media

This section works the same as we saw in the Summary and Job Positions.

10.1.9 Sharing and Saving

As you can see, in every section, we can indicate if we want to openly publish the changes we've done, for our level 1 contacts to know, or not to post it, if we leave it deactivated.

Now all we have left is to click "Save" and gradually introduce the rest of our studies.

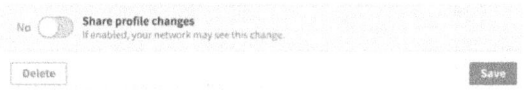

10.2 I Can't Find my University

If you can't find your University in the list, the easiest thing you can do is going to the University's website and, on the website's top or bottom, you'll find the LinkedIn icon. There, you copy the name as it's written, and when you enter it, it will appear on the list. https://www.linkedin.com/school/15106496/

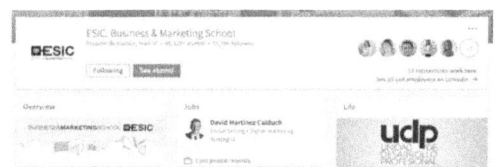

If you can't find it in the website, contact them directly.

Chapter 11

Profile – Skills and Validations

The professionals who have skills in their LinkedIn profiles receive 13 times more profile visits in average than those who don't have any.

- *LinkedIn*

We can say without a doubt that we're before one of the most important blocks, and which may have the most impact on your LinkedIn profile.

In this section, we're going to indicate which are our skills and abilities; what can we do.

Currently in the CVs, in the formation part (which is very important), the weight of the "what can you really do" section is increasing, companies are making a shift in the way to conduct interviews and analyze professionals.

"The school record is useless"

- *Laszlo Bock, Google's Human Resources Vice president*

Laszlo Bock's full notice.

https://www.elconfidencial.com/alma-corazon-vida/2013-06-28/el-expediente-academico-no-sirve-para-nada-asegura-el-responsable-de-rrhh-de-google_501910/

Since LinkedIn introduced the option of validating skills and abilities of other professionals (which must be your level 1 contacts) in September 2012, by 2016 over 2 billion validations were done.

Skills validations are a good way of acknowledging your level 1 contacts' skills, those you know to be true. They'll also allow your level 1 contacts to validate yours. If well used, they can help you create your professional brand

People who have at least 5 skills set, receive at least 17 times more visits to their profile.

- LinkedIn

When we talk about abilities and skills, we have to differentiate between the hard and soft. On one side, you're going to gain office automation knowledge, advanced Excel, etc. and, on the other hand, teamwork, conflict management, etc.

Chapter 11: Skills and Validations 161

Next to each skill, you'll see that a number appears. That number is the amount of people who have indicated you know about that topic. The maximum number that appears is 99.

> *Eight of the 10 skills that have gained to most popularity in the classification in 2013-2014 aren't technical, and nearly half of them were related to health.*
>
> *- LinkedIn*

11.1 Previous Work

Before writing everything you're good at, let's plan ahead and make a previous work to do it right.

To start, c'mon, I mean you ;-), making a list of at least 15-20 words that describe what you know to do, always from a professional point of view. The more you have, the better. Maximum is 50.

1	11
2	12
3	13
4	14
5	15
6	16
7	17
8	18
9	19
10	20

Chapter 11: Skills and Validations

Think in what you know en in what do you want to be located.

Make a list of your functions in each one of your positions.

Detail the applications you know how to use: Office, G-Suite, SolidWorks, InDesign, SAP, Salesforce, Hootsuite, Zoho, Google Ads, etc. Skills: Team management, closing sales, etc.

Visit several professionals like yourself, to see what are the ones they've put up. Those you know, you can enter them if you're interested, and those you don't can give you an idea of what you should learn.

Be very strict and enter only that which you really know. I recommend, for starting, you enter 15-20, and the first 5 must be arranged in importance order.

11.2 Adding the Section

If you can't find this section in your profile, you can add it. When you enter your profile, on the top right you'll see this blue button.

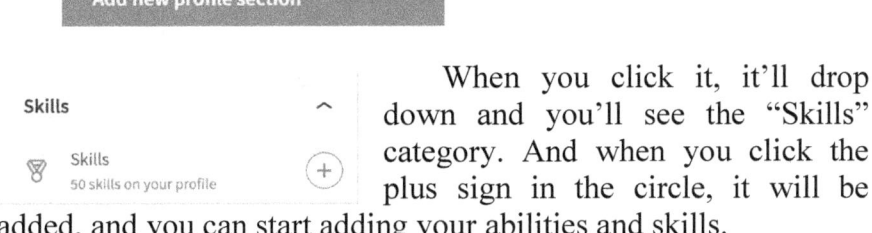

When you click it, it'll drop down and you'll see the "Skills" category. And when you click the plus sign in the circle, it will be added, and you can start adding your abilities and skills.

11.3 Adding Skills, deleting them and Arranging them

Another section that has received lots of changes has been this one. As you can see, now only the first three skills/abilities are shown, and on the right side, the people who have validated it appear (only level 1 contacts), indicating you're good in that skill/ability.

If we click on see more, it'll drop down and appear as you can see in this image, all the skills with its validations.

Chapter 11: Skills and Validations

11.3.1 Adding Skills

On the top right of the Skills sections you'll see the phrase "Add a new skill".

Add a new skill ✏

By clicking it, a screen to add them will appear. As you type the word, LinkedIn searches for skills and abilities to make it easier for you, you can select them among the results, or write whatever you want.

11.3.2 Rearranging

Add a new skill ✏

By clicking the blue pencil on the top right, a screen with the list of words you've introduced will appear. On the right side of the list you'll see a stripes icon for every word. Clicking it and dragging up and down, you can change their order.

Reorder

11.3.3 Eliminating Skills

To remove any of the skills you've entered, you must click the blue pencil, and when it appears on the list, on each term's left, you have an X. Remember, there's no Undo, and if the validations made from people are lost, they cannot be recovered.

✕ **Social Media Strategist** · 59

✕ **Hootsuite** · 86

11.3.4 Configuring Validations

Pressing the blue pencil in the Skills and Validations section, on the screen where the list of all our skills appear, below everything on the left side, we have this option.

Adjust endorsement settings

This function allows us to configure the way we're going to let our skills be validated. By clicking on it, we reach this screen.

Endorsements ✕

Manage how you receive and give endorsements

I want to be endorsed — Yes

Include me in endorsement suggestions to my connections — Yes

Show me suggestions to endorse my connections — Yes

The three options shown are:

I want to be endorsed	I recommend you activate this option, because the number of validations in each one of the skills.
Include me in endorsement suggestions	LinkedIn, in an automatic way, shows the skills of your level 1

Chapter 11: Skills and Validations 167

to my connections	contacts. Asking you to, if you know they're good at it, validate them. With this option we ask LinkedIn to show us to our level 1 contacts, so they validate us.
Show me suggestions to endorse my connections	So, LinkedIn shows us skills of our level 1 contacts, to be able to validate them.

As a bare minimum, you should have the first one activated. In my case you can see I have all three activated.

11.3.5 Who has Validated me, and Hiding it

Next to the skill, besides the number, a photo of the person who validated us is shown. We can, on one part, know exactly which people have validated us and, also, we can control who we want to be shown and which not, with the possibility of hiding them.

Being in the section of Skills and Validations, we click on one of our skills. In this case, I'll do it with Hootsuite.

Hootsuite · 86

By clicking on the name or the number, this screen will appear, which represents all the people who have validated this skill.

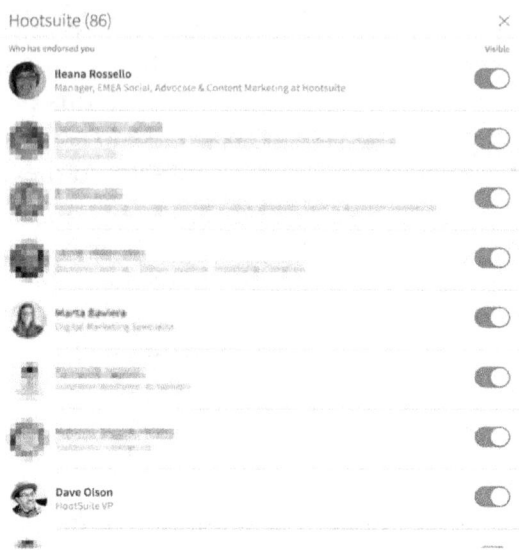

Next to each name, you'll see a blue button to make that person visible, or to hide it.

11.4 Statistics

With the objective of giving you the biggest possible amount of data and information, and not making a full chapter here, full of data and more data which, besides, you must necessarily continually update, I've created a note in Evernote for you to access every infographic and data on LinkedIn skills latest tendencies.

https://www.evernote.com/pub/davidmcalduch/linkedinskillsandendorsements

To be able to access, you don't need to be registered in Evernote. Entering from your browser you can access the information I leave there, and every time you enter, you'll have the latest version of what I've included.

Chapter 11: Skills and Validations

If you want to register in Evernote (it's free), you can do it from here www.solucionafacil.es/elefante and that way, you'd have an updated copy of the information in your computer, smartphone or tablet, of all the material I store there.

The data I've gathered will come really good for you, since you'll have the tendencies of which are the most demanded skills, on a global level and by country. You must keep in mind that they're not the same in every country, and you must analyze the country where you are or the one in which you want to work.

These are the ones I've included in the Evernote note (you'll see there are two specific to job searching):

- Fastest growing skills 2014-oct
- 25 most powerful skills in 2014
- The 25 most important abilities to be hired in 2017
- Millions of validations in under 6 months 2013-Feb
- The 25 skills that can help you get hired in 2016

11.5 Managing from a Smartphone
11.5.1 Validating Skills

With the new versions of the LinkedIn App, among their numerous improvements, now we can validate our contacts' skills. We open the app in our smartphone, and we enter the profile of one of our level 1 contacts.

We click on "See 7 more skills".

And this screen will appear with the full list.

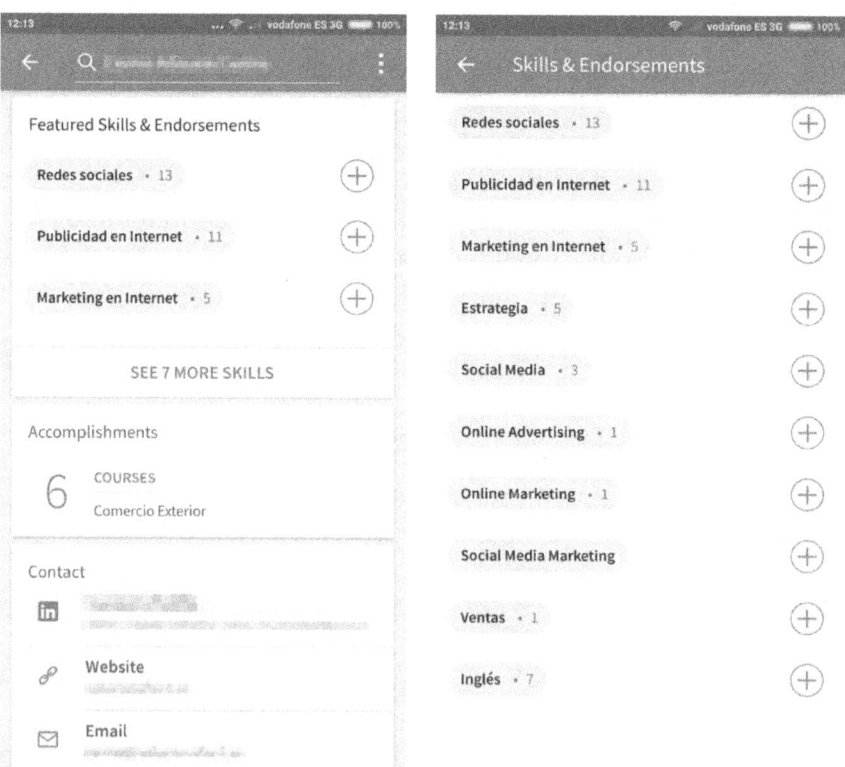

To validate skills, we can do it in any of the two screens, touching the circled +, and we can validate as many as we want.

Chapter 11: Skills and Validations   171

11.5.2 Managing our Skills

With the LinkedIn App, you can do everything we've seen about skills and validations: registering them, rearranging them, deleting them, etc.

We enter our own profile and we go down until we see the section.

We click on see more.

This screen will appear with the list of all our skills. We click on the white plus sign we have on the top right corner. It allows us to add new skills, and the blue pencil is for managing them. By clicking the blue pencil, we'll go to a different screen.

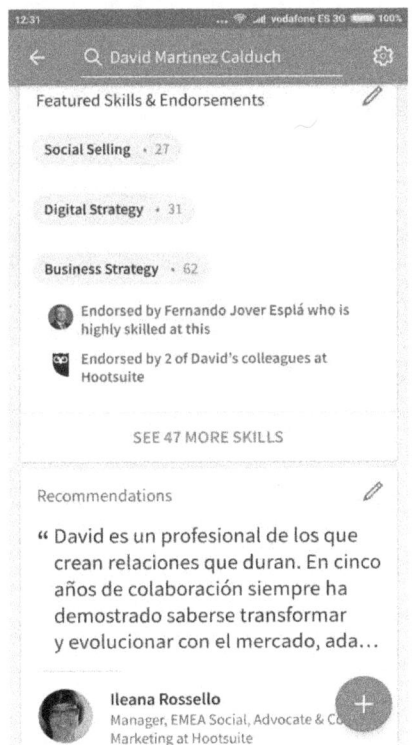
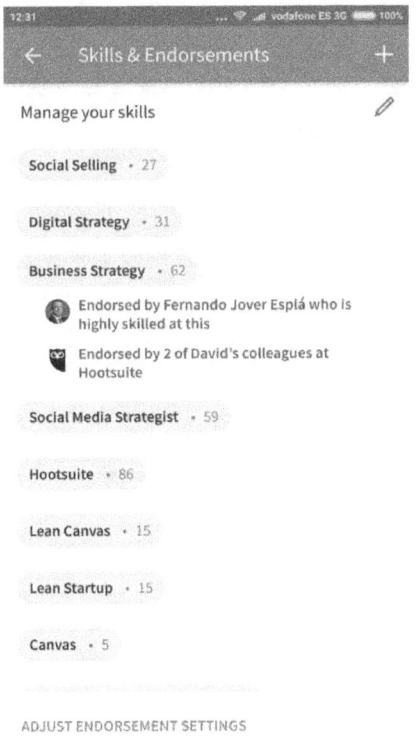

When this screen appears, we can delete what we don't want, and rearrange them.

In every screen, you'll see that the option "Adjust endorsement settings" is below everything, which will take you to this screen that we've already seen.

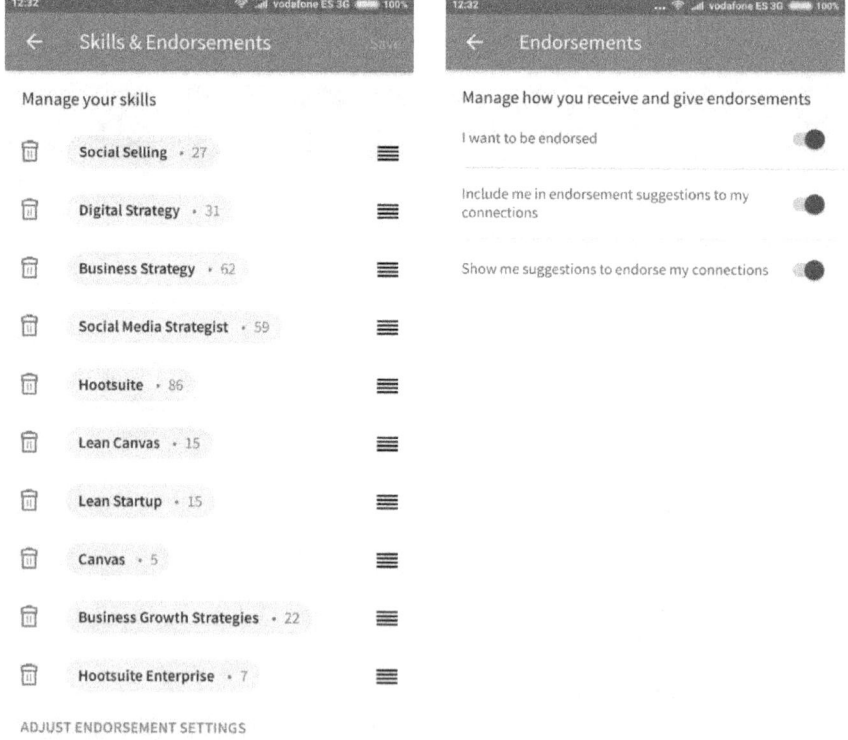

11.6 Job Search

> *Recruiters allocate 60 seconds to read the skills and validations.*
>
> *- LinkedIn*

This section we're seeing, is very important for providing valuable information for recruiters. Truly focus in the skills you want to highlight, remember that less is more.

Indicate in which ones you're good, and capable of adding value. Of course, you have to be able to prove it.

Check the Evernote note I shared with you, where you have a lot of data related to which skills are more powerful, and which are the most searched I your country.

Here you have the most important skills on a global level for people looking for a job, now you have to see which the ones for your country are.

The Top Skills of 2016 on LinkedIn
Global

#	Skill	Change	#	Skill	Change
1	Cloud and Distributed Computing	0	6	Network and Information Security	+1
2	Statistical Analysis and Data Mining	0	7	Mobile Development	-1
3	Web Architecture and Development Framework	+6	8	Data Presentation	NR
4	Middleware and Integration Software	+1	9	SEO/SEM Marketing	-5
5	User Interface Design	+5	10	Storage Systems and Management	-2

11.7 Preventing Someone from Validating us

There's not a specific function to prevent a person from validating us. The only way of doing it is that they're not a level 1 contact of ours.

For that, we have two possibilities:

1. Hiding your validations, as you've already seen.
2. Eliminating them from your contact list.

In order to eliminating someone from your contact list (they won't get any notification) you must follow these steps:

2.1 In the upper menu we go to Network click it.

2.2 In the left side of the screen appears the amount of contacts we have, we click on "See all".

10,815
Your connections
See all

2.3 A list with our contacts will appear. On every contact's right side we have a button to send them a message, and another button with three dots. If we click on that button the option "Remove connection" will show.

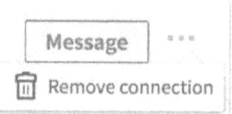

11.8 Doubled Validations

People, in a proactive way, may validate you on the skills you've entered, but they could also suggest new ones, and sometimes it can occur they duplicate.

It's not possible to merge two skills, meaning, if we have two equal skills, and we have validation from several people on them, we have to decide which one to keep, and eliminate the other losing those validations.

If you don't want to lose any validations from the two (repeated) skills, there's nothing you can do but keeping both.

11.9 Validating and de-validating

To validate a person's skills (they have to be our level 1 contact), we only have to go to their profile (desktop, smartphone, or tablet), search for the Skills section, and click on the plus symbol to validate, and if we click in any of the validations, we de validate it.

Chapter 12

Profile – Recommendations

Let your clients speak for you.

Getting recommendations, I'll anticipate you, is a very complicated job. But as benefit of the effort, I can assure you that the positive impact it can have on your profile is worth the work it takes to get them.

What better way for someone to inform themselves about you than when visiting your profile, they're able to read how your clients feel about you? As you can see, it shows the person's photo, full name, and position.

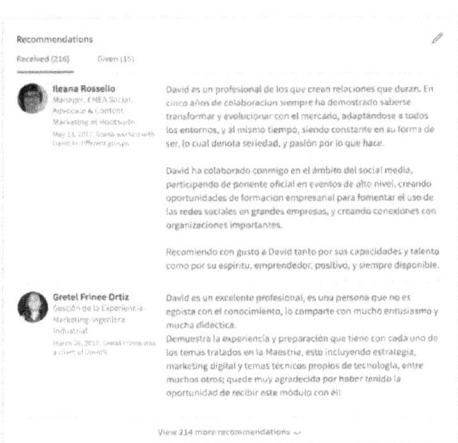

12.1 You Lie more than a LinkedIn Recommendation

I'm guessing the title of this point caught you by surprise, but the most important thing is to leave things crystal clear, and that you're aware of what we've got in our hands.

What we're working on here is your professional career, and what you do or don't do is your absolute responsibility.

There're people who, in their pursuit to accelerate their professional career, invent stuff. There're people who falsify university degrees, etc. and of course, there are people who get imaginative with recommendations. The use you give to this fabulous tool is up to you

12.1.1 The Bad Use of Recommendations

How do you feel about a false CV? How would you feel about that person? And, how would you feel about a professional who plays around with recommendations?

I've seen professors giving LinkedIn lessons, and at the end of the session, telling students he's going to make a recommendation for each one of them because that always goes well in a profile. For shame.

From whom can you NOT ask a recommendation:

- Your subordinates, since you're in a position of power, and therefore these recommendations won't be believable.
- Your partners, nor them to you. It'll seem like you're playing cards.

This is one of the many examples I've been seeing on my own but, as I told you, it's your professional career and each one of us demonstrates who we are with our actions.

Chapter 12: Perfil – Recommendations

12.1.2 The Good Use of Recommendations

How do you feel about a profile where clients give their opinion about that person?

From whom can you ask a recommendation:

- Your clients, they hold the pan by the handle, and can therefore give their opinion freely.
- Your team chiefs, and your bosses. For the latter, the protocol is to ask the recommendation when you've left the company.

Be careful when asking a recommendation from your boss, since the first thing they'll think is that you're leaving the company.

12.2 How to Request One Step by Step

To ask for a recommendation we must follow these steps:

- We can only ask a recommendation from people who are our direct contacts (level 1). It goes without saying, they have to be registered to LinkedIn.
- We must visit their profile, and on the top right of the screen, there's an icon formed by three dots. By clicking it, a menu is shown, and the second to last option is "Request a recommendation".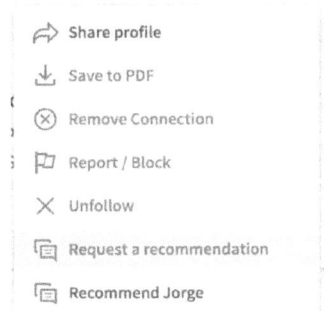

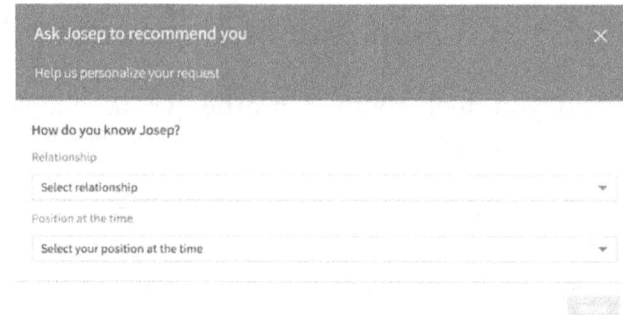

- Now what we need to do is indicate which type of working relationship we had.

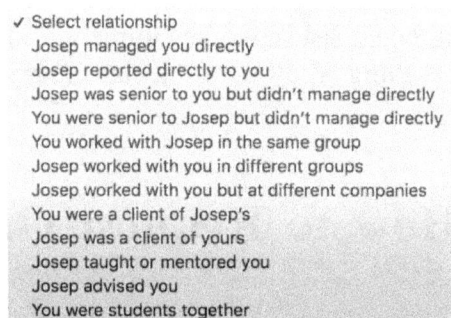

- And in which job position that person was when we coincided.

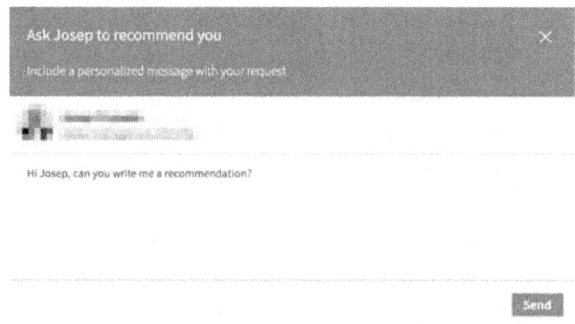

- And now we must detail for which we want to be recommended.

It's important to specify about which project, what we did (which is for what they have to recommend us).

12.3 How to do a Recommendation

In this life you have to be generous, and if you've worked with any professional deserving recognition for their labor, it's important to publicly acknowledge it. It's not about handing out recommendations for anyone but do it for those people who actually deserve it.

When you visit a profile, in the same button where you ask for a recommendation, in the last option we can make one, which will be delivered to the person.

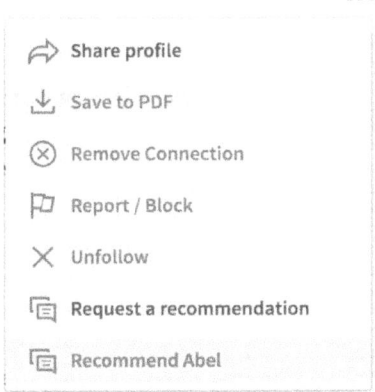

Important:

- Do the recommendation only if their performance was model, not only for doing their job.
- Be honest and say exactly why you recommend that person.
- Say nothing but the truth. When in doubt, don't do it.

12.4 Managing Recommendations

In the recommendations section, we have those we have received, those we have made for other people, and on the right side we have the blue pencil.

12.4.1 Received

When we click it, this screen will appear.

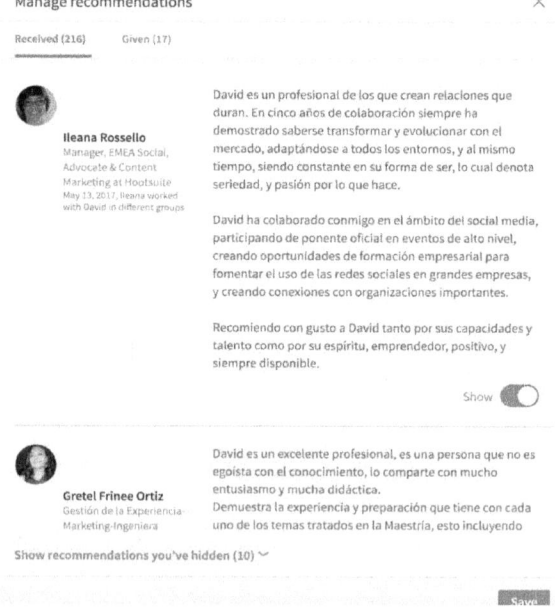

Here you have the recommendations people have made for you, and under each recommendation, on the right side, you can make that recommendation be visible in your profile or not.

Chapter 12: Perfil – Recommendations

12.4.2 Given

If we click on "Given", we can also manage the recommendations we've done.

Manage recommendations   ×

Received (216)   Given (17)

Clara Piqueras
Comité organizador del IV
Simposio Internacional de
Innovación Aplicada
July 2, 2017, David managed
Clara directly

He trabajado durante un año con Clara en IMAT, es una persona muy trabajadora, ha asumido las responsabilidades necesarias para llegar a los objetivos, y se ha formado en las herramientas y plataformas que han sido necesarias para el proyecto. Agradecerle todo el trabajo realizado y felicitarla por su gran dedicación.

Delete   👁 Visible to: Public

Olga Maturana Domínguez
Comité Organizador IV
Simposio Internacional de
Innovación Aplicada (IMAT
2017)
July 1, 2017, David managed
Olga directly

He tenido la oportunidad de trabajar con Olga durante un año en IMAT y ha demostrado ser una persona muy volcada en su trabajo, ha asumido todas las funciones y responsabilidades que se le han asignado, siempre dispuesta a aprender y tomar la iniciativa. Estoy seguro que tendrá un gran carrera.

Delete   👁 Visible to: Public

In each recommendation we've given, we have the control to be able to delete it, and on the right, we can indicate if we want the recommendation to be shown in our own profile.

👁 Visible to: Public

These visibility settings will only affect how recommendations appear on your own profile.

Only you

Your connections
Only LinkedIn members directly connected to you.

Public   ✓

12.7 Moving Recommendations

Recommendations go linked to a job position or study, so, if we eliminate that job position or that study, the recommendation is left orphaned.

To reassign the recommendation, you must enter Modify Recommendation, and then you select which position or study it belongs to.

12.6 Difference between Validations and Recommendations

A skill validation is a way in which your level 1 contacts can validate the skills you've put in your profile with a click, when they know you're good. It's very fast and easy.

And a recommendation is a piece of text written by that person where a positive comment about you appears, accompanied by their picture and position. We can also request those.

Chapter 13

Profile – Accomplishments

> *35% of professionals feel uncomfortable when explaining their achievements.*
>
> *- LinkedIn*

It can't be no other way; this section has also gone through major changes. The biggest of all is that now every block is shown together in just one place called Accomplishments, as you can see below.

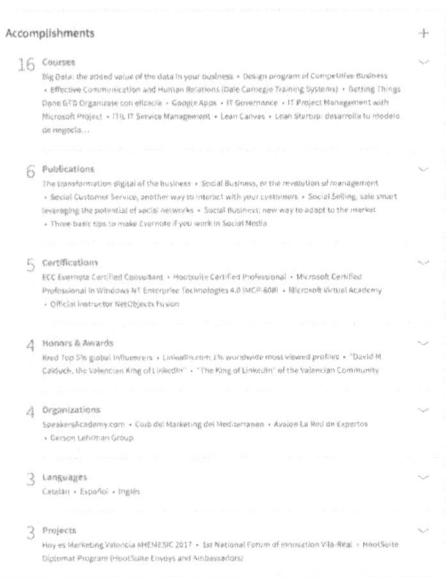

13.1 How to Add Accomplishments Sections

On the very top of our profile page, on the top right, we have a button for adding more sections.

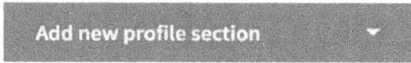

By clicking the button, three blocks will drop down, and inside each one of them, we have different options to add to the accomplishments section.

Chapter 13: **Profile – Accomplishments**

Now you only need to click on the plus sign, next to the achievements section to add it.

Another way of adding more modules in the Accomplishments sections.

My recommendation is that you add all you can.

13.2 Courses

This is how the courses module looks now.

If we click on the top right arrow, the module drops down and looks like this.

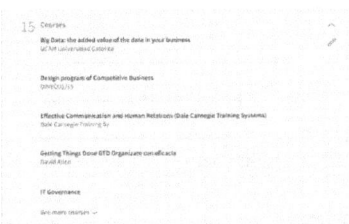

Following the same functioning than the rest of the sections we've seen so far, by dropping down it only shows 5 courses, and to see 5 more you have to click on the text on the bottom, "See more courses".

13.2.1 Adding Courses

We click on the "Accomplishments" plus sign, and we select "Course".

By clicking on "Course", this screen for adding the new course appears.

Course name: self-explanatory

Number: if the course has any kind of code or number

Associated with: if it's related to any job position, for example, a course that the company has made internally

"Share profile changes", if you want to notify your level 1 contacts when you add this course. When you add a course, it is placed last.

13.2.2 Modifying Courses

Next to each course, when you place the cursor on top, you'll see a blue pencil appear on the right side.

And by clicking it, the course sheet appears so we can modify it.

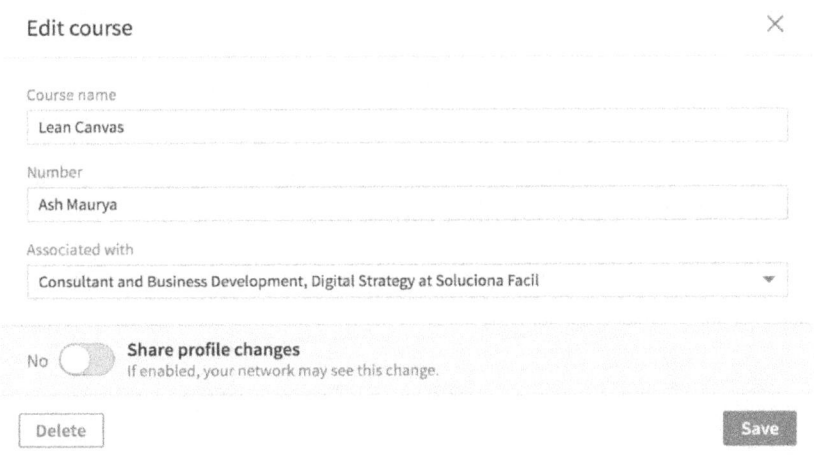

When we're done, we click "Save".

13.2.3 Eliminating Courses

Next to each course, by putting the cursor on top, you'll see a blue pencil appear on the right side, and after you enter the course sheet, below everything on the left side, you have the "Delete" button.

13.2.4 Arranging Courses

There's not an option for arranging courses.

13.3 Publications

In this module you can register the publications you've done, and the offline/online medium where you've published them.

13.3.1 Adding Publications

On the "Accomplishments" section, we click on the blue plus sign, and we select "Publication".

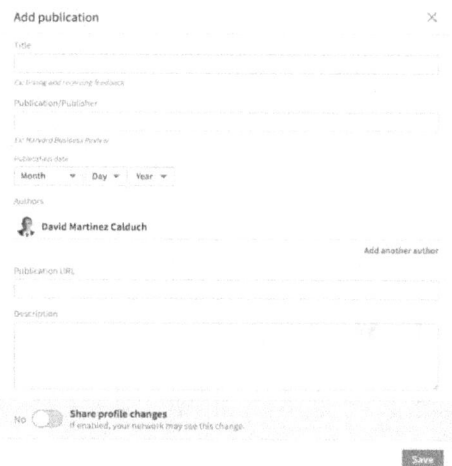

Now we must gradually introduce every field: the title of the publication, in which means it has appeared, the date it was published, if we did it with other people, the URL of the publication, the description explaining what we've written in the publication, and the rest of the options are the same as in Courses, if we want to notify our level 1 contacts when it's published, then we click on Save.

13.3.2 Modifying and Eliminating Publications

Edit publication   ×

Title
Three basic tips to make Evernote if you work in Social Media
Ex: Giving and receiving feedback

Publication/Publisher
Blog Oficial Evernote España
Ex: Harvard Business Review

Publication date
July   30   2014

Authors
David Martinez Calduch

Add another author

Publication URL
http://blog.evernote.com/es/2014/07/30/tres-consejos-basicos-para-aprovechar-evernote-si-trabajas-en-so

Description
EverNote as a CRM system.
For those who engage in social media as a freelancer, CRM (Customer Relationship Management) is an essential piece in his work. The part of commercial activity is 50% of the work of a freelance. In my company we use CRM level work management team for customer management, monitoring of commercial actions

No   **Share profile changes**
      If enabled, your network may see this change.

Delete   Save

The functioning is exactly the same as the one we've seen on Courses.

13.3.3 Changing the Order of the Authors

In LinkedIn's previous version (before 2017), the order could be changed, but now it can't.

13.4 Certifications

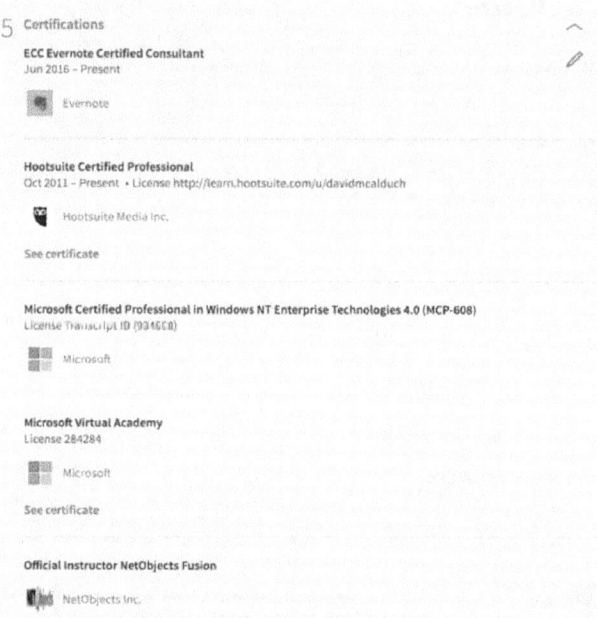

Here we will register those certifications we have. We can include the certification's ID and even the URL. The functioning is the same as in Courses and Publications.

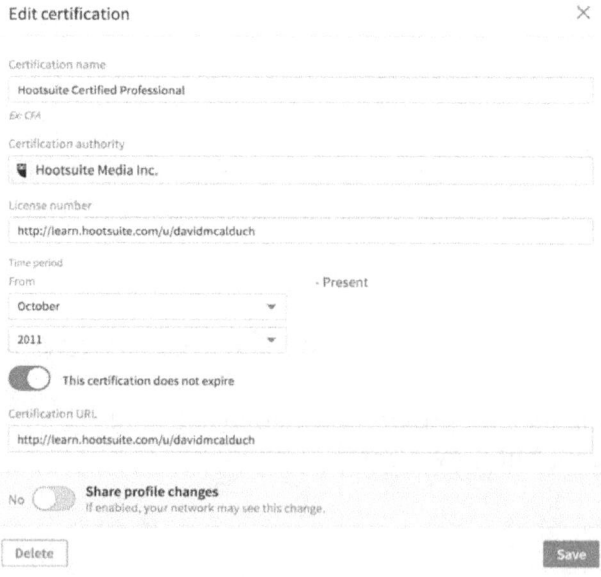

Chapter 13: **Profile – Accomplishments**

13.5 Honors and Awards

In this section you must register those awards and acknowledgements you've achieved.

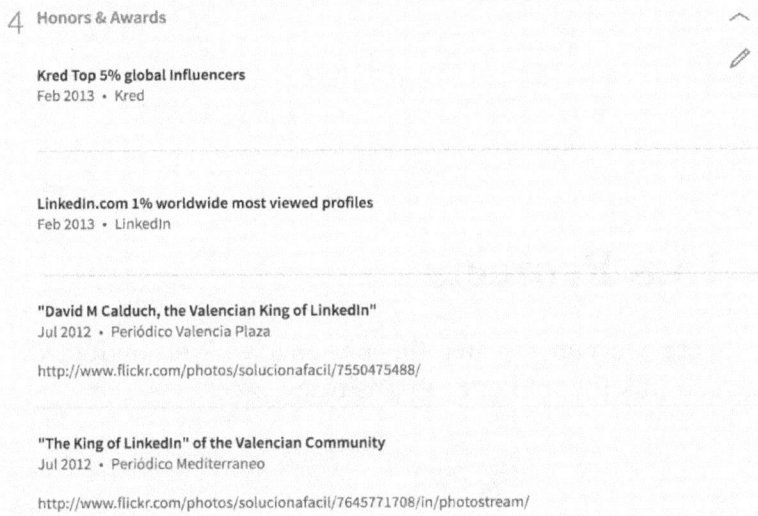

13.6 Organizations

Here you can add those associations and organizations to which you belong.

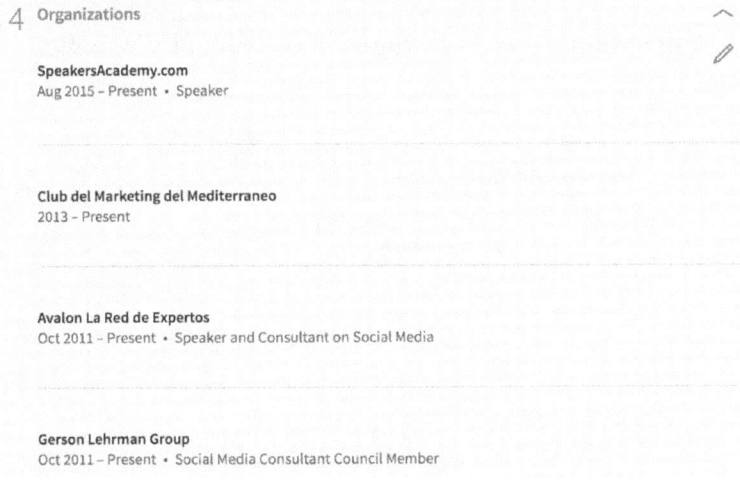

13.7 Languages

Here you can indicate which languages you know and the level you have in each one of them.

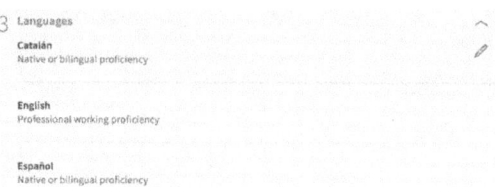

13.8 Projects

Here we can register the projects we've conducted, and we can also link them to our job positions.

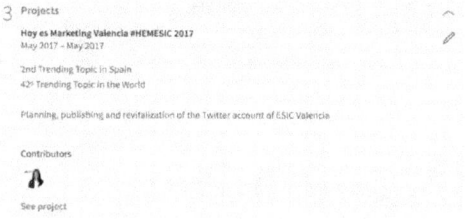

13.9 Patents

In this module you can register any patent you have.

Chapter 13: **Profile – Accomplishments** 195

13.10 Test Scores

In this module you can register the test scores you want to be known.

13.11 Volunteering

In this module you can detail your Volunteer Experience.

13.12 Interests

Here we can manage who/what we follow, for their posts to appear on our wall.

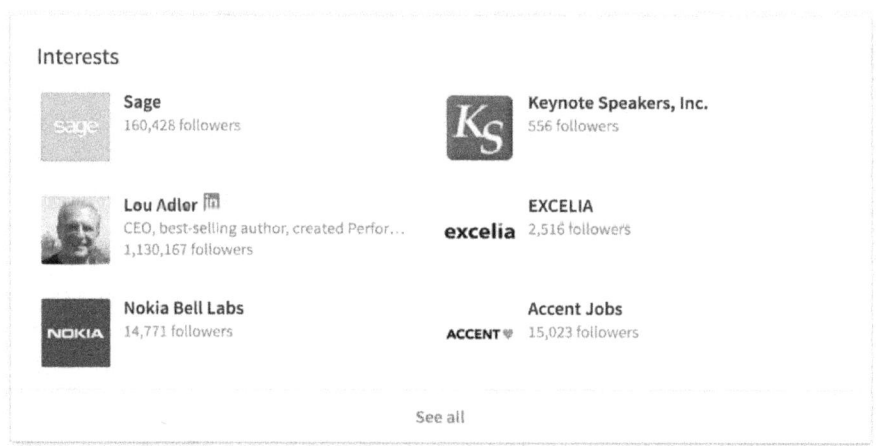

Clicking on "See all" we see four categories: Influencers, Companies, Groups, and Universities, and we have the button for unfollowing them.

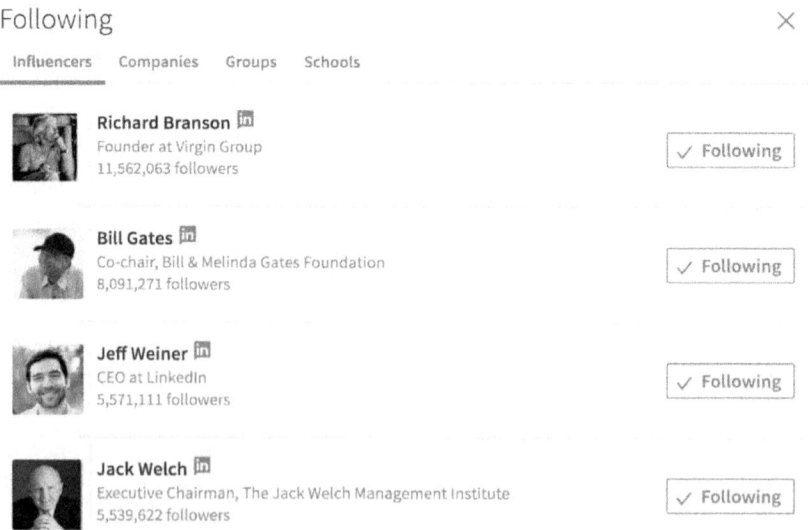

Chapter 14

Profile in Several Languages

If you're thinking of positioning yourself on an international level, to do business, finding a job, etc., my advice is that you do your profile in every language you know, with English as the bare minimum.

14.1 Available Languages

Currently, LinkedIn allows us to create our profile in 19 different languages. Below, you can see my profile in Chinese and Russian. In total, I have it in 5 languages, including English, Spanish, and French.

Here you can see my profile in Chinese

https://www.linkedin.com/in/davidmcalduch/?locale=zh_CN

Here you can see my profile in Russian

https://www.linkedin.com/in/davidmcalduch/?locale=ru_RU

These are the available languages to create your profile.

- ✓ Choose...
- Arabic
- Bahasa Indonesia
- Chinese (Traditional)
- Czech
- Danish
- Dutch
- German
- Italian
- Japanese
- Korean
- Malay
- Norwegian
- Polish
- Portuguese
- Romanian
- Swedish
- Tagalog
- Thai
- Turkish

Chapter 14: Profile in Several Languages

14.2 Creating your Profile in another Language

When we're on our profile page, on the top right there's a drop-down menu where we have the languages in which our profile is available, in my case, Spanish, Chinese, Russian, French, and English. The last option is adding another language.

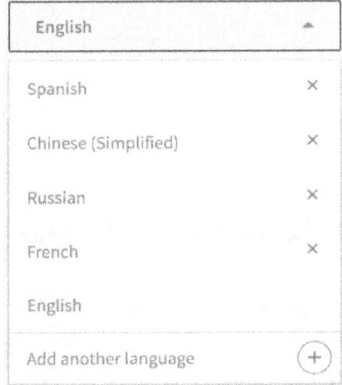

By clicking "Add another language", this screen appears.

We have a drop-down menu called "Language" to select in what language we want to create it, including the 19 languages I commented.

Indicating which language, we want, "Deutch" (German) for example, it creates the profile with the whole structure we have done, positions, studies, etc. but everything blank, and it's us who must fill it in German.

Besides, to add to insult to injury, the LinkedIn Profile is something that is alive and we're continually updating, which multiplies the work, since we have to repeat this update in each one of the languages.

14.2 Eliminating Languages

In the same drop-down menu, in the right part we see the X that allows us to delete the language. Remember there is no Undo button and the information written in that profile will be totally lost.

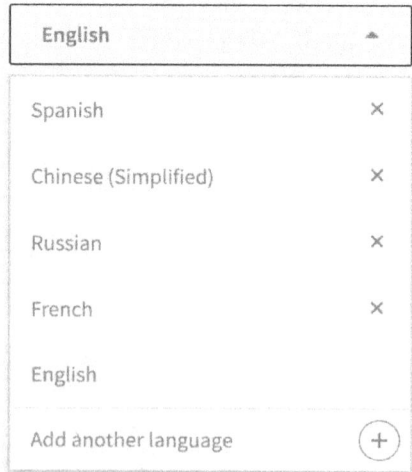

Chapter 15

Types of Premium LinkedIn Accounts

There are many types of Premium (paid) LinkedIn accounts, everything you've seen in this book so far is possible within the free version.

Now let's see the types of Premium accounts there are, and what's the target of each one of them. Up next, you have the URL where LinkedIn has the information of all the types that exist.

https://www.linkedin.com/premium/products

Within each one of them, there are 3 or 4 variants.

LinkedIn has created a page for managing every service of the Premium account you have hired. To access it, you must go to the top right menu where your photo appears, and after clicking it we select "Access My Premium".

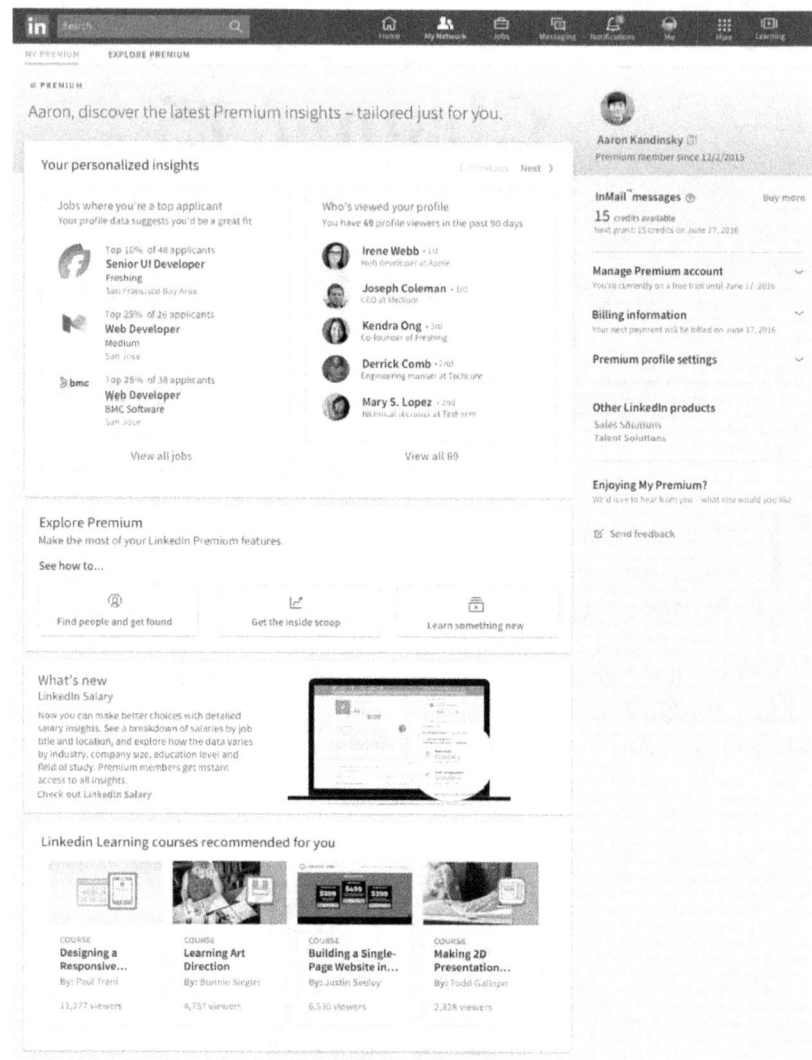

Regardless of the Premium version you hire, if you don't do a good job with your profile, you're going to lose opportunities.

15.1 Job Search

One of the Premium account types, is one specific for people in a job searching situation.

Premium Career functionalities:

- According to LinkedIn's statistics, people with this account type are hired twice as fast in average.
- 3 InMail messages a month to be able to contact recruiters, even if they aren't your level 1 contacts.
- Access to complete statistics (90 days and how they found you) of who has seen your profile.
- Appearing as a featured Candidate in recruiters' search results.
- Appearing above everything on the candidates list.
- Access to statistic information of the candidates that have signed up for the job positions.
- Comparative between you and other candidates.
- Online video courses.
- One free month, the basic account is 26.61 €*/month.

15.2 Companies

This account is intended for professionals who want to generate a contact network and do businesses.

Premium Business functionalities:

- According to LinkedIn's statistics, professionals with this account type get 6 times more profile visualizations in average.
- 15 InMail messages a month.
- Access to complete statistics (90 days and how they found you) of who has seen your profile.
- Extended information of company profiles, the company's growth, and its tendencies, including hiring.

- Unlimited profile visualizations.
- Access to every profile in searches, even 3rd grade.
- Online video courses.
- One free month, the basic account is 42.34 €*/month.

15.3 Sales

This account is specific for salespersons, and in it we have access to LinkedIn's sales tool, Sales Navigator.

Sales Navigator Professional functionalities

- Salesmen with this account, if they also use the Social Selling methodology, are 3 times more likely to surpass their quota, according to LinkedIn.
- 20 InMail messages a month.
- Access to complete statistics (90 days and how they found you) of who has seen your profile.
- Information about sales.
- A wall besides LinkedIn's own wall, where you only see your Leads and the contacts with whom you're working, with their posts, media appearances, job changes, company growth, etc.
- Unlimited profile visualizations.
- Access to every profile on searches, including 3rd grade.
- Premium search with Lead Builder.
- Go straight to those responsible for the decision making, create lists of possible contacts with the advanced search filters.
- Recommendations of possible clients and saved contacts.
- Quickly discover de right people and save the names to keep up to date with them.
- One free month, the basic account is 58.07 €*/month.

15.4 Hiring

This account is for recruiters.

Recruiter functionalities:

- Access to Recruiter Lite
- 30 InMail messages a month to contact candidates.
- Message templates.
- Access to complete statistics (90 days and how they found you) of who has seen your profile.
- Advanced search
- Go straight for the best candidates with advanced candidate search filters designed for personnel selection.
- Unlimited profile visualizations.
- See profiles through search results with no limits, as well as suggested profiles, even 3rd grade ones!
- Smart suggestions.
- Use dynamic suggestions when searching to discover more candidates.
- Automatic candidate following.
- Make a following of candidates and openings with Projects.
- Integrated hiring.
- Manage the list of candidates from a single place.
- Specific design for personnel selection.
- Enjoy a LinkedIn with functions for personnel selection.
- After a free month, pay the reasonable price of 90.69 €*/month, if billed annually.

More information on Recruiter Lite https://business.linkedin.com/talent-solutions/recruiter-lite/tour

More information on Recruiter https://business.linkedin.com/talent-solutions/recruiter/product-tour

Chapter 16

Job Search

86% of those who make hiring decisions agree that it's important for candidates to clearly communicate their achievements.

- LinkedIn

The way of finding a job has radically changed. It's not only about contacting recruiters, and applying to job offers, but we must also create a professional brand (profile), and be active (publications, networking, and interactions).

16.1 Being on the Search without my Boss Knowing

90% of professionals are open to new opportunities.

- LinkedIn

When I impart my training sessions for Managers and Businessmen, and the discussion if an employee can be in a job search situation arises, I always say, who do you think wouldn't switch jobs if they offered them double their salary right now? Everyone is on a job search, what changes is the intensity level of that job search in that person.

That said, the most important thing is for the employees to be comfortable, and for them to want to be in the company they're in. And, for the time they're there, that they do their work in the best possible way.

From the employee's point of view, in case you want to appear on the recruiters' searches, but you don't want your profile to show you're in a job search situation, LinkedIn has created this page.

www.linkedin.com/jobs/career-interests

In this screen you can write a note that recruiters will be able to see, indicating which spots you're open to, in which locations, contract types, and in which sectors.

16.2 How Many Job Offers Are There

> *There are more than 6 million job positions published in LinkedIn Jobs.*
>
> *– LinkedIn*

These are a few, and the quantities, of the available positions:

1. Cloud and Distributed Computing Skills (1,000+).
2. Statistical Analysis skills (nearly 10,000) and Data Mining (nearly 12,000).
3. Web Architecture and Development Framework (35,000+).
4. Middleware and Software Integration (10,000+).
5. User Interface Design (3,000+).
6. Network and Information Security (7,000+).
7. Mobile Development (nearly 6,000).
8. Data Presentation (nearly 1,000).
9. SEO/SEM Marketing (43,000+).
10. Storage Systems and Management (32,000).

Now what you need to do is to enter LinkedIn's job offers searcher, make searches to know the amount of active job offers there are for the position you're looking for.

16.3 Analyzing Salaries

LinkedIn has a fabulous tool which indicates us the real salary for each job position. Unfortunately, it's only for the Anglo-Saxon world. I'll leave it here for you to check.

https://www.linkedin.com/salary

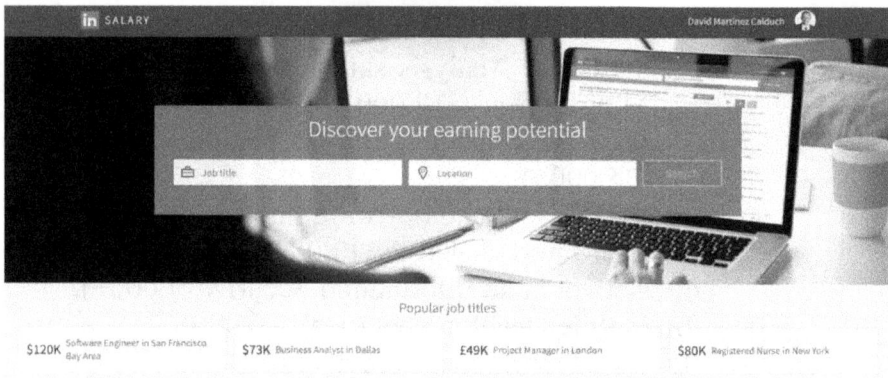

If you're having doubts about studying languages, take a look at the salaries and all your doubts will be cleared.

If you're thinking of taking an international leap in your career, this tool will come in handy.

Chapter 17

Safety and Privacy

With the latest changes introduced in LinkedIn's platform, a great job has been done to simplify the management of every security option.

In this chapter, we're going to review the most important ones for you to decide how you want them to act, depending on your strategy.

17.1 How Other People See Me when I Visit Them

When you visit any person, it initially indicates it's us. Likewise, if we visit our profile visit statistics, we'll see the people who has visited us.

In a computer, by going to www.linkedin.com on the left section we see this box.

By clicking on "Who's viewed your profile" this screen appears.

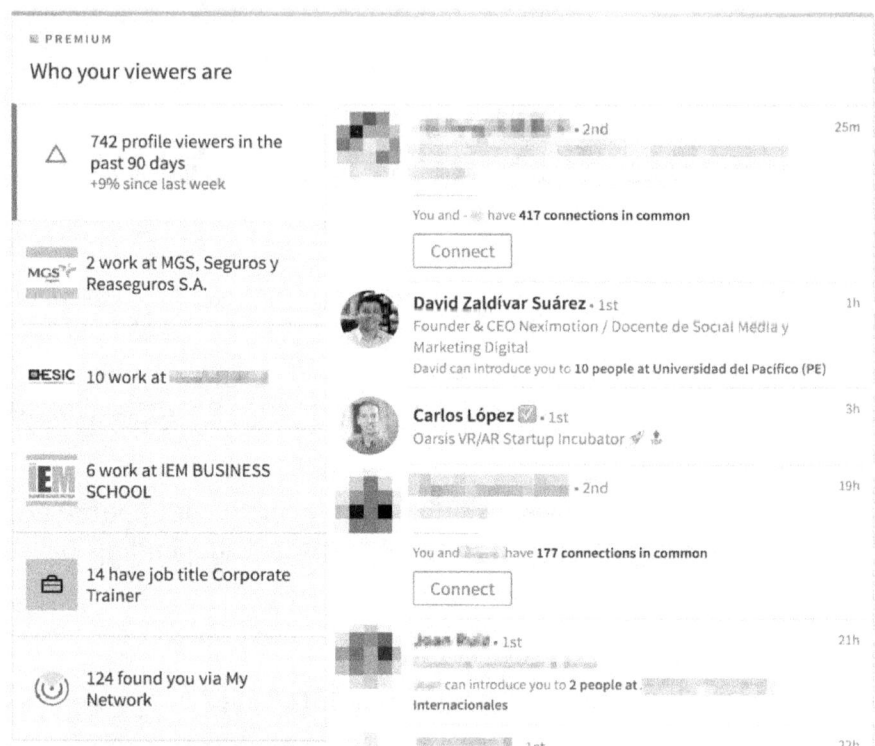

You can see on the right section how the people who has visited my profile can be seen: photo, full name, position, and company.

When you visit other people, they'll see you in that very same screen, when they enter their "Who's viewed your profile", but there are some situations where it's possible you need to visit profiles without people knowing it's you. First let's see how to do it, and then we'll see what we might need this for.

Chapter 17: Safety and Privacy   213

To be able to configure if we want to be seen or not when we visit other professionals, we must go to the menu on the top right, where we have our picture, and after we click it, we select "Settings & Privacy".

After we enter the screen, in the central part, we have this menu, we select "Privacy".

Account   Privacy   Communications

And on the central part of the screen, the following options will be shown.

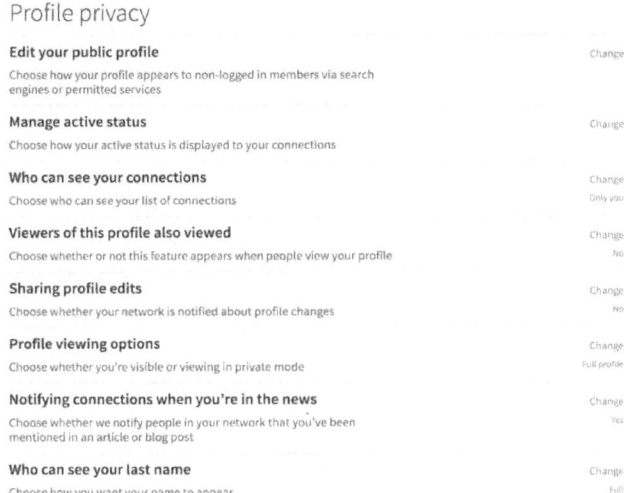

We select the sixth option, "Profile viewing options", we click the name and the three options will drop down.

Profile viewing options — Close
Choose whether you're visible or viewing in private mode — Full profile

Select what others see when you've viewed their profile

Your name and headline

David Martinez Calduch
Social Selling • Digital Marketing Strategist - MBA
Valencia Area, Spain | Online Media

Private profile characteristics

Salesperson in the Marketing and Advertising industry from Valencia Area, Spain

Private mode

Anonymous LinkedIn Member

Let's see each option, what they're for, and what they imply.

1. It's the one I have selected, when I visit someone, the other person sees all my data, and if they wish, they can visit my profile to know more about me. Since I give that information to other people, LinkedIn, in return, also gives it to me, which is the screen we've seen before, who's viewed your profile.
2. Neither the photo nor the name is shown, and the access to your profile is not allowed. Your position is shown in a generic way, in my case it says "Salesperson", the sector and the location, in my case Valencia Area, Spain. In return of not letting the people you visit know it's you, LinkedIn kindly eliminates all the visits and you can't see who visits you.
3. It's the highest level of anonymity, it says a member of LinkedIn has visited you, but nothing else can be known, even if the other person has a Premium version, they'll see the same thing. As you can imagine, LinkedIn also eliminates the visits to your profile.

The usage I give to it, as you can see, it's for other people to know I've viewed them, I don't have any issue with that.

I do have clients who have requested, how to be able to visit the competition, without they are knowing it's them, and that's when you have to use the options 2 or 3; I'd say 3.

These anonymous visit options (2 and 3), are used when I work with recruiters. They come great for them to visit the candidates, avoiding the candidates knowing the recruiter is visiting, and from which company.

In case you're going to use options 2 or 3, my advice is that, since LinkedIn will delete the visits you've had, before activating those options, check the visits, and then activate the option and use it. Once you finish, activate option 1 again so you can have statistics from new visits generated from that moment.

Selecting any of the three options will be automatically saved, there's not a save button.

17.2 Access to your Contact List

Initially, LinkedIn, in good faith and with the objective of generating opportunities, configured the access to our public contact list for our Level 1 contacts.

The reason is very simple, according to LinkedIn's policy, we must only accept those people we know, therefore, since we know them and accept them, they have our trust and there's no problem with them being able to see our contact list.

That said, I'm going to give you the example of my situation, so you can see another point of view. I use LinkedIn very intensively for my work, and I have a lot of clients on my LinkedIn contact list so, leaving my contact list open is leaving my work contact list open. On the other hand, I'm a person who's open to accept other professionals in my contact network, I always offer the benefit of the doubt. Then, people always demonstrate who they really are.

For this reason, I've had my contact list blocked for several years now. Having done that, I assure you, has brought me a lot of discussions where people told me I was doing a lot of networking, but I had my list blocked.

My response has always been the same, and it's the one I'm going to give to you: This is about Businesses, and if you need me to explain more, then we're not on the same wavelength. As it's usually said, a word to the wise.

With this I don't mean you have to block your list, I'm just showing you two ways of seeing it. The decision about your situation is yours. I'm going to show you how to do it, in case you need to block it, or unblock it.

We're still in the same screen as in the previous point, and now we'll select the third option "Who can see your connections".

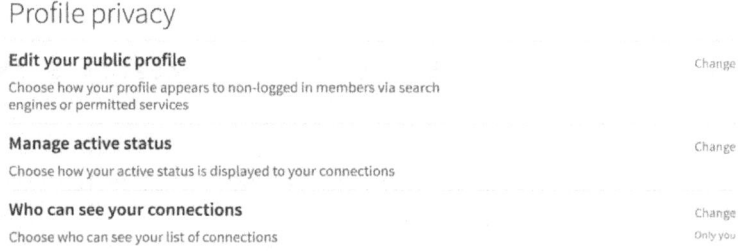

And by clicking on the title, it drops down and we can select two options, only you or your contacts (Level 1).

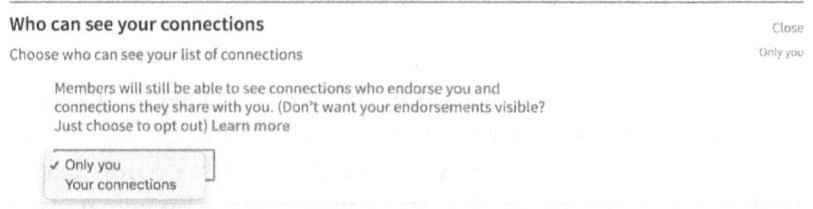

17.3 Other Profiles like Yours

Once again, with the goal of helping us and helping others, LinkedIn, when you visit a profile, on the right side of the profile, other professional profiles that have been visited when that profile was visited are shown.

Let's see an example, we visited the profile of ESIC Valencia's General Director, and on the right side we can see other profiles, which have also been visited when that profile was visited. You may see that many ESIC employees appear. This could be a useful usage to leave activated.

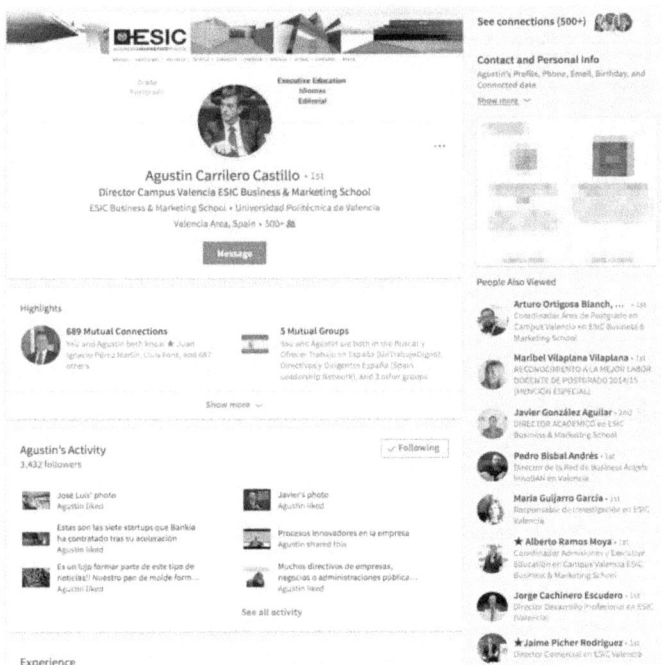

If you visit my profile, you'll notice I also have it deactivated. The reason? I understand it can be useful to locate other people but, based on my strategy, when someone comes to see my profile, it's for that, to see my profile. To look for other profiles there are already searches. But as I tell you, it's a personal vision based on my strategy.

And now we're going to see how to activate and deactivate this block of information, which is only visible when your profile is visited from a computer.

We're still in the Privacy screen, and we select the fourth option, "Viewers of this profile also viewed".

Profile privacy

Edit your public profile — Change
Choose how your profile appears to non-logged in members via search engines or permitted services

Manage active status — Change
Choose how your active status is displayed to your connections

Who can see your connections — Change
Choose who can see your list of connections — Only you

Viewers of this profile also viewed — Change
Choose whether or not this feature appears when people view your profile — No

We click on the title and the option to activate or deactivate drops down.

Viewers of this profile also viewed — Close
Choose whether or not this feature appears when people view your profile — No

Should we display "Viewers of this profile also viewed" box on your Profile page?

No

17.4 In which Devices do you have LinkedIn Connected

LinkedIn offers us the opportunity of managing in which computers, tablets and Smartphones we have open sessions with our LinkedIn account.

It's not about becoming paranoid, but it's interesting and recommendable to sign out of those sessions you're no longer using, or for example, your work computer LinkedIn session when you're on vacation, or those devices you no longer use.

While in the "Settings and Privacy" screen, in the central menu we select "Account".

Account   Privacy   Communications

On the left part we have a menu, and we must select the first option, "Basics".

| Basics
Partners and Third parties
Subscriptions
Account

And when we enter we have these options, we must select the sixth one, "Where you're signed in".

Basics

Email addresses Change
Add or remove email addresses on your account 12 email addresses

Phone numbers Change
Add a phone number in case you have trouble signing in 1 phone number

Change password Change
Choose a unique password to protect your account Last changed: March 11, 2017

Language Change
Select the language you use on LinkedIn English

Name, location, and industry Change
Choose how your name and other profile fields appear to other members

Where you're signed in Change
See your active sessions, and sign out if you'd like 11 active sessions

We click on the title and a list of all the sites/devices where we've logged in with our LinkedIn account will drop down. If we logout, when we try to reenter LinkedIn with that device/browser, the only thing that will happen is that it'll ask for our email and password again to authenticate us and preventing a foul use of our profile.

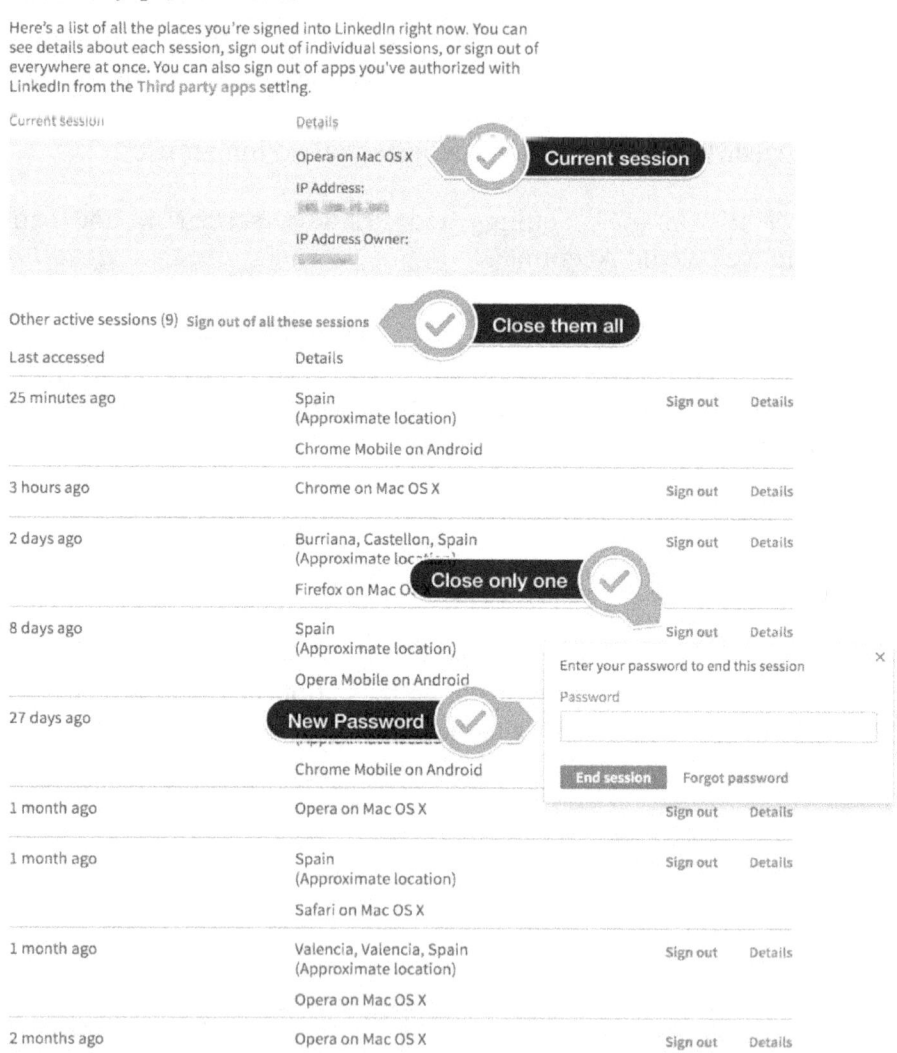

Above everything in grey color, we can see our current session. Then, it indicates us we have 9 more sessions open. If you

Chapter 17: Safety and Privacy   **221**

click on that option, we can close them all at once. Then we have the list of every session, and we can click on the right of each one of them and close the ones we want. It'll always ask for our LinkedIn password as a security measure.

17.5 Where is my LinkedIn Account Connected

Many apps and websites allow us to sign up using our LinkedIn account, and also to be able to import data from our profile or contacts to save us work.

LinkedIn has an option where we can check where we've connected our LinkedIn account, and thus being able to revoke the access.

We're still in the "Settings and Privacy" screen, on the central menu we're on "Account".

Account	Privacy	Communications

And on the left menu, we select the second option "Partners and Third parties".

Basics

| Partners and Third parties

Subscriptions

Account

On the screen's central part appear these options, we select the first one by clicking on the name.

Partners and Third parties

Permitted Services — Change
View services you've authorized and manage data sharing — 80 connected apps

Twitter settings — Change
Manage your Twitter info and activity on your LinkedIn account — Connected

WeChat settings — Change
Link, remove, and control visibility of your WeChat account — Connected

And a list will drop down, of all the sites where our LinkedIn account is connected. In my case, it indicates I have it connected to 80 services/apps.

To remove that connection, it's as easy as clicking on "Remove". It's recommendable to eliminate the connection with everything you no longer use, as a security measure.

Chapter 18

Frequent Problems and their Solutions

18.1 I Want to Close a LinkedIn Account

These are the steps to follow.

1. You must go to the top menu where your photo is, and we select "Settings & Privacy".

2. We enter the upper menu "Account" and the right menu "Account".

3. At the end of it, we'll find the option "Closing your LinkedIn account".

Account

Closing your LinkedIn account   Change
Learn about your options, and close your account if you wish

The moment you deactivate your account, all the data is erased. It's better if you download a security backup of all the data.

18.2 My Company Profile is a Professional Profile

The use of a Professional Profile to create a company's digital presence is forbidden by LinkedIn's usage rules, which means you can't use a Professional Profile to create a Company Profile. In fact, LinkedIn can delete your profile for breaching the rules.

In this case, you must either delete it, or convert in the Professional Profile of a Manager or any other Director, if they still don't have one, with the objective of not losing the contacts.

18.3 I Have Two Accounts and I Want to Merge Them

LinkedIn has created a function that allows it to merge two professional LinkedIn accounts, in case we've signed up twice. That way, we can merge the contacts of both accounts.

To close your LinkedIn account from the **Adjustments and Privacy** page:

Chapter 18: Frequent Problems and their Solutions

1. Click on the Me icon, on the top part of your LinkedIn home screen.
2. Select "Settings & Privacy" on the drop-down menu.
3. We enter the top menu "Account" and the right menu "Account".

> Account
>
> Basics
> Partners and Third parties
> Subscriptions
> | Account

4. And select the last option of the screen.

Merging LinkedIn accounts   Change
Transfer connections from a duplicate account, then close it

5. You can also do it by entering directly to this link.

   https://www.linkedin.com/psettings/account-management/merge-connections

6. Mark the reason for closing your account and click on **Next**.
7. Introduce your account's password and select Cancel Account.

18.4 I Forgot my Password

In case you don't remember the password to enter your LinkedIn account, you can request for it to be reset through this URL.

https://www.linkedin.com/uas/request-password-reset

They'll ask you to introduce the email you used to sign up to LinkedIn, and they'll send you an email with a link. I am opening it; a new window will open and you'll be able to create a new password.

If you don't receive the email, check the Spam folder.

If it still doesn't arrive, wait a few minutes. If it still doesn't arrive, it's possible you didn't sign up with that email.

18.5 I don't remember the Password and can't Access my Email

18.5.1 Using another Email

The only way LinkedIn has to send you the password, is to the email you used to sign up, or you can try to have it sent to another of the emails you've registered in your profile. (See "8.6 emails").

Chapter 18: Frequent Problems and their Solutions

18.5.2 Verifying your Identity

If there's no way to access any email you've listed on your LinkedIn account, the only solution is to make an identity verification request. You must go to this link.

https://www.linkedin.com/uas/request-password-reset

You're going to need:

- A Smartphone, or a computer with a webcam.
- Your driver's license, national identity document, or passport.
- An email address where you can be contacted.

The documentation you grant them is deleted by LinkedIn within 14 days. You'll be asked to photograph your documentation and associate it to an email where they can contact you.

In the page you must click on «I don't have Access to my email».

They'll ask for a new email address, and then they'll ask for a valid document (passport, official ID document). From there, they will contact you to continue the procedure.

18.5.3 Renewing the Password via Mobile

Another option you have is that, if you've entered your phone number, you can do the password change through an SMS the same moment you ask for a password reset.

https://www.linkedin.com/uas/request-password-reset

18.5.4 Configuring a Mobile

To configure your phone to be able to use this option in the future, you must go to this address.

https://www.linkedin.com/psettings/phone

Phone numbers   Close

Add a phone number in case you have trouble signing in   1 phone number

Phone numbers you've added

ES +34 ██████████   Make primary   Remove

☑ Use for password reset

Add phone number

18.6 I don't want my Profile to be Public

In the same way we can make our profile be public, we can make it stop being public. You just need to follow these steps:

To show or change your public profile:

1. Go to your profile
2. In the right part go to "See your public profile"

Edit your public profile

https://www.linkedin.com/public-profile/settings

3. Mark the first option for your profile to not be publicly visible.

○ Make my public profile visible to no one
◉ Make my public profile visible to everyone

4. And now click on "Save"

Save

Chapter 19

Last Tips

I hope you've followed my advice and applied what we've continually been learning in the book. If you have, now you can use this book as a consultation book.

If you liked this book, I encourage you to give your opinion in Amazon http://amazon.com/author/davidmcalduch

And, if you want to continue moving forward with your knowledge, you can continue with the rest of the books in the series: https://thekeysof.com/linkedin/

www.ingramcontent.com/pod-product-compliance
Lightning Source LLC
Chambersburg PA
CBHW050205230526
45470CB00001B/250